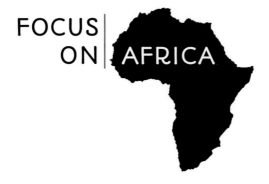

FOCUS
ON AFRICA

Politics in Contemporary Africa

Bridey Heing

Cavendish
Square

New York

Published in 2017 by Cavendish Square Publishing, LLC
243 5th Avenue, Suite 136, New York, NY 10016

Library of Congress Cataloging-in-Publication Data

Names: Heing, Bridey, author.
Title: Politics in contemporary Africa / Bridey Heing.
Other titles: Focus on Africa.
Description: New York : Cavendish Square Publishing, 2017. |
Series: Focus on Africa | Includes bibliographical references and index.
Identifiers: LCCN 2016028968 (print) | LCCN 2016029639 (ebook) |
ISBN 9781502623812 (library bound) | ISBN 9781502623829 (ebook)
Subjects: LCSH: Africa—Politics and government—1960– |
Political culture—Africa.
Classification: LCC DT30.5 .H44 2017 (print) | LCC DT30.5 (ebook) | DDC
320.96--dc23
LC record available at https://lccn.loc.gov/2016028968

Editorial Director: David McNamara
Editor: Caitlyn Miller
Copy Editor: Michele Suchomel-Casey
Associate Art Director: Amy Greenan
Production Coordinator: Karol Szymczuk
Photo Research: J8 Media

Printed in the United States of America

Contents

Protests are common across Africa. Here, people take part in a 2012 demonstration against increased oil prices in Lagos, Nigeria.

A Continent of Change

Africa is a large, diverse continent stretching from the Mediterranean Sea in the north to the southern Atlantic Ocean below the equator in the south. It is made up of fifty-four countries, the most countries on any one continent, and is home to numerous ethnic groups, languages, and traditions. Each country also has unique and complex **politics**, with varied concerns, government structures, and relations.

As part of the "global south," a term used to refer to Southern Hemisphere regions that receive little international attention, Africa is often mistakenly discussed as if it were one country. This hides the rich history and diversity that make the continent unique and erases its cultural and political differences. The politics of Morocco, for instance, where a monarch rules the state along with an elected parliament, and South Sudan, one of the newest independent countries in the world, are extremely different from one another. Some African states are democratic, some are ruled by kings, some are controlled by dictators, and many are divided by conflict. Africa is a vibrant continent, and politics there are no less complex than those of Europe or Asia.

Although culturally and politically diverse, African states' political history have a lot in common. The continent was subjected to the slave trade, with millions of men, women, and children taken to work in North America and Asia. Africa was also colonized by European powers, with the British, French, Italians, and Dutch all holding significant territory and others controlling smaller areas. Colonization was a violent, oppressive system, in many cases making Africans second-class citizens in their own countries. Most African states became independent in the second half of the twentieth century. In states like Rwanda, tribal rivalry led to violent civil war and **genocide** as postindependence **power vacuums** tore countries apart. Elsewhere, such as in Swaziland, **absolute monarchy** replaced the absolute rule of the colonizing forces.

Colonization had a large impact on African politics, shaping the way central government looks in most states. Before colonization, few African states had central governments in the way we think of them. Instead, affairs were governed by tribes, with many individual tribes existing within each area. These groups negotiated land holdings, resource sharing, alliances, and conflict. But under colonization, tribal leaders were stripped of all authority, and each country was run by a representative of the occupying country's government. When granted independence, many countries struggled to establish stable governments, and in some cases conflict has continued until today.

According to the African Union, an organization that facilitates cooperation among member states, Africa is divided into five subregions. Northern Africa stretches across the top of the continent, and its politics are shaped by its close association with the Middle East. Western Africa, along the Atlantic, has long struggled with instability, disease, and insecurity. Central Africa, located in the center of the continent, has been dominated by conflict and authoritarian rulers. Eastern Africa, along the Indian Ocean, has seen some of the most significant conflicts of the twentieth century but is also home to stable states. The region also struggles with terrorism. Southern Africa, at the very bottom of the continent, has struggled with **corruption** and civil war, as well as the legacy of **apartheid** in South Africa. The only African state that is not part of the African Union is Morocco, which is part of northern Africa.

In this book, each chapter focuses on the politics of one subregion, exploring the recent political history of each country and the way the states interact with each other. African countries face many challenges, including poverty, terrorism, and conflict. Yet the future looks bright as Africans around the continent come together to make their voices heard.

The Arab Spring, which included protests in Cairo's Tahrir Square, led to the resignation of Egyptian president Hosni Mubarak.

1 | Northern Africa

According to the African Union, northern Africa includes Egypt, Libya, Tunisia, Algeria, Morocco, the Sahrawi Republic, and Mauritania. Although overlap does exist, this classification is different from North Africa, which is frequently referenced in relation to the Middle East and does not include Mauritania or the Sahrawi Republic. Northern Africa is made up of three smaller geographic subregions: the Maghreb, the Sahara, and the Nile Valley.

The political history of northern Africa has been influenced heavily by invasion and conquest. In the seventh century, northern Africa became part of the large Muslim empire centered in the Middle East and later the Ottoman Empire centered in modern-day Turkey. In the nineteenth century, however, the region was colonized by European powers, including Italy, France, Spain, and Great Britain. It wasn't until the early to mid-twentieth century that the countries of northern Africa were able to secure independence and establish their own governments.

Since then, the region has undergone significant changes and has seen vast political evolution. Ruled primarily by dictators and **authoritarian** rulers until 2011, the **Arab Spring** protests of 2011 started in Tunisia before spreading to Egypt and Libya, as well as Syria and the Middle East. Today, the region is in a state of transition, with some states coming out of the protests as fledgling democracies while others, such as Libya, have struggled to find stability as warring **militias** battle for control.

In this chapter, we'll take a closer look at the legacy of colonialism, some of the key political issues in the region, and the ways political powers within northern Africa interact with one another—and countries around the world.

UK prime minister Winston Churchill visited Egypt in 1943. By that year, Egypt was independent but continued to be influenced by the British government.

Colonization

Northern Africa was dominated by the Ottoman Empire until the 1800s, when British powers took control of the region.

There was a diverse European presence in northern Africa, with the British, French, Italians, and Spanish controlling areas at various times.

Egypt

Occupied in the late 1880s when economic hardship made the country vulnerable, Egypt was a British **protectorate** until 1922. That year the country was declared independent, but Britain maintained influence until 1956, when a military **coup** replaced the pro-British president Muhammad Najib with nationalist Gamal Abdel Nasser. His presidency established a trend of authoritarian governance, in which the president has ultimate power over the state.

Libya

Libya was part of the Ottoman Empire until 1911, when it became an Italian colony. The Italians held control, despite rebel groups challenging them, until the Allied forces pushed Italy out during World War II. The British and French divided the country into regions of influence, and the two powers remained in the country until 1951. That year the monarchy, under King Idris, took over governance.

Tunisia

A former French protectorate, Tunisia became an independent state in 1956. Tunisia, like other regional countries, was dominated by strongman politics for most of the twentieth century. This means that the country was ruled by a series of leaders who wielded complete power; sometimes the term "strongman" is used as a synonym for "dictator." Habib Bourguiba became the country's first leader after having started the independence movement in the early 1930s, and although he took the title of president, he was an authoritarian ruler. Power passed from Bourguiba to General Zine El Abidine Ben Ali in 1987, when Bourguiba was found unable to rule due to medical concerns. Ben Ali, although supportive of reforms early on in his presidency, adopted the same style of dictatorial rule as Bourguiba-era authoritarianism when unrest led to demonstrations in 1989. Staged elections maintained his control on the government for over twenty years until Tunisia became the first state to witness mass protests as part of what became known as the Arab Spring.

Algeria

Algeria was a French colony until 1962, when it won its independence after an eight-year war that killed more than one million Algerians. But following independence, the country struggled to find balance between warring factions. Instability escalated in the late 1980s, with the assassination of leading opposition figure Ali Mecili. After years of unrest, civil war broke out in 1992 when military officials intervened, fearing **Islamists** would win that year's national elections. The military government declared emergency law, and the country descended into a conflict that the international organization Human Rights Watch declared a human rights crisis.

Morocco

Before becoming independent in 1956, control of Morocco was divided between the French and the Spanish. Spain controlled a coastal protectorate, which it continued to occupy until 1975. France held the rest of the country. When the French left Morocco, the country established a form of government called a parliamentary monarchy. Yet decades of conflict with Algeria and Mauritania over the status of the former Spanish territories along the coast followed. These conflicts, along with domestic conflicts among the government and opposition factions, caused instability.

Mauritania

A French protectorate until 1960, Mauritania is one of the largest countries in Africa, but it is 90 percent desert. After independence, the first president, Moktar Ould Daddah, established a one-party state under the constitution, setting a precedent for authoritarianism. A bloodless coup put in place a military government, which continued the authoritarian trend in Mauritanian politics with harsh crackdowns on **dissent**.

Government Structures

Northern Africa is in a state of transition, with three governments overthrown since 2011 and significant reforms implemented in another. As a result, the government structure of each state is extremely unique. In Tunisia, a parliamentary presidential republic—with an elected president and parliament—has emerged from years of negotiation between political factions. But in Egypt, the first democratically elected government to follow the 2011 revolution was unseated in a military coup. Although the government is elected by popular vote, politics are still dominated by one ruler. In Libya, as of this writing, central governance has broken down almost completely, with two rival governments set up and negotiations on unification stalled.

In Mauritania, power passed to Colonel Maaouya Ould Sid'Ahmed Taya in the early 1980s, and he maintained tight control of the government but allowed some space for opposition political factions. Political parties were legalized in 1991, but President Ould Taya held on to power through elections until 2005, even as opposition parties gained local and national representation. That year he was unseated in a military coup. Under Colonel Ely Ould Mohamed Vall, who was put in place as the president, a **referendum** in 2006 found that 97 percent of Mauritanians favored a constitution that limited presidential terms. In response, Vall agreed to step down and allow democratic elections to take place. Those elections were held in 2007 and were Mauritania's first multicandidate presidential elections. But in 2008, another military coup unseated the democratically elected government. General Mohamed Ould Abdel Aziz became president, winning an election in 2009 that many alleged lacked credibility.

Although political parties are able to operate in Mauritania, the regular coups and unrest that have plagued the country mean that the political system is underdeveloped. The latest elections, held in 2014, were boycotted by most opposition parties in protest of Abdel Aziz's tight control on politics. Competition within the state's security forces and tension with the military has further undermined stability. In 2012, the attempted assassination of Abdel Aziz caused unrest and underlined divisions among the government's leadership. Ethnic divisions also undermine the government. Haratin and Afro-Mauritanians together make up 70 percent of the population, but the minority Bidhans hold almost all the top offices in the government and military. There are tragic class divisions along ethnic lines; despite abolishing slavery in 1981, the practice continues with no real consequences. The Global Slavery Index estimated in 2014 that around 140,000 people were enslaved in the country. The Haratin are considered a lower class than other ethnic groups, and the majority of slaves are from this population.

Algeria and Morocco did not experience revolutions and are both ruled by strong central governments. In Algeria, a dictatorship was established after a seven-year civil war, with the military playing a prominent role in politics. In Morocco, the monarchy responded to protests in 2011 by introducing limited representative government. A power-sharing arrangement was established between the king and the leading Islamist opposition party.

Moroccan politics also highlight an element of a healthy democracy that many states have struggled to embrace postindependence: pluralism. Pluralism means that power is not held by a single leader or group. Rather, a pluralistic political system is influenced by many groups that are able to express their unique viewpoints. For much of the twentieth century and into the twenty-first century, politics in northern African states—and in some cases politics on the continent more broadly—did not allow for pluralism to take root. Leaders relied on political **repression** to maintain their own power, not allowing opposition groups to flourish or only making room for groups that were ultimately loyal to the system and did not challenge the ruler's authority. In many cases, this kind of repression erupted into conflict (as seen in Libya when once-sidelined factions tried to fill the post–Muammar Gaddafi power vacuum).

But in the case of Morocco, the process of opening up the political system to new voices has begun. While it will take time for power to be equally spread across parties and institutions, pluralism is crucial to a vibrant and healthy state.

Sahrawi Republic

The Sahrawi Republic is a largely disputed coastal area once held by the Spanish. When the Spanish left the area in 1975,

The flag of the Sahrawi Arab Democratic Republic, a state in the Western Sahara not recognized by most of the world

Morocco, Algeria, and Mauritania claimed the territory, also called the Western Sahara. The following year, independence group the Polisario Front declared the Sahrawi Arab Democratic Republic (SADR) in the same territory. After decades of conflict, a cease-fire was signed between all parties in 1991. Morocco controls the bulk of the territory, while the Sahrawi government controls some land along the eastern border, which is called the Free Zone.

The Sahrawi Republic has not been recognized as an independent state by the United Nations, and only a handful of individual governments have recognized it. The African Union, which facilitates relations between African states and the international community, made the SADR a full member nation in 1982; Morocco left the organization in protest and has not rejoined since.

The SADR government has most authority in refugee camps, located in western Algeria. There the government works with international organizations and administers aid. Its lack of recognition by the international community has meant that it is largely unable to take part in international commerce or affairs. The SADR also has no economic infrastructure, with Morocco controlling most of the economy in the territory to the west. The United Nations Security Council established the United Nations Mission for Referendum in Western Sahara in 1992, with the goal of conducting a referendum among the Sahrawi to determine their future. But the Moroccan government has refused to agree to terms that would allow a referendum to take place.

The Arab Spring

In 2011, Tunisia became the first state to witness mass protests as part of what became known as the Arab Spring. In December 2010, a street vendor named Mohamed Bouazizi protested harassment by the authorities in the city of Ben Arous by setting himself on fire, and his death led to a widespread uprising across the country. Protesters demonstrated against high unemployment, corruption, lack of democracy, and human rights violations. By mid-January, 2011, Ben Ali was forced to resign and leave the country.

Soon, Arab Spring protests were sweeping the region. In Egypt, protests were in response to long-time political repression, economic inequality, corruption, and lack of democracy. In 1981, Hosni Mubarak became president after the assassination of Anwar Sadat. Mubarak remained president through staged elections and oppression of dissidents. He was forced to resign in early 2011. But since Mubarak stepped down from office, those problems have not been fully addressed.

An interim government was formed after Mubarak left office, and the following year elections were held for both the parliament, or People's Assembly, and the presidency. The Muslim Brotherhood, an Islamist party, won both the presidency and a majority in the People's Assembly. The new president, Mohamed Morsi, had run on a platform of moderation and nationalism, but soon after he took office many feared he was consolidating power in his and his party's hands. He stayed in office for one year; in 2013 a military coup ousted him and suspended the new constitution. In 2014, one year after the coup, military officer Abdel Fattah el-Sisi, who had taken office on an interim basis, was elected president.

In Libya, a military coup unseated King Idris and replaced the monarchy with an authoritarian dictatorship led by Colonel Muammar Gaddafi (sometimes spelled "Qaddafi" or "Kadafi") in 1969. Gaddafi ruled Libya for more than four decades until a revolution unseated him in 2011. When protests broke out against Gaddafi's rule that year, he did not step down like Tunisia's Ben Ali or Egypt's Mubarak, both of whom had been unseated in Arab Spring protests. Instead, he responded with a violent crackdown against demonstrators. Armed militias started forming to fight against the government's forces, with many aligned as much along tribal lines as against Gaddafi. In the aftermath of the revolution, that **tribalism** has led to an ongoing power struggle, undermining the democratic aspirations of the early demonstrations.

Also in 2011, Moroccans took to the streets to demand democracy and social justice. The current monarch, King Mohammed, responded by initiating reforms to strengthen the parliament with a new constitution. That same year, national elections saw a significant victory for the Justice and Development Party (PJD), a moderate Islamist political party. The party's leader, Abdelilah Benkirane, was appointed by the king to head a coalition government in 2012.

Since then, a power-sharing arrangement has helped establish some reforms in Morocco. But many scholars aren't overly impressed by the progress, pointing out that ultimate power is still held by the king and that the PJD was already willing to cooperate with the monarchy before sweeping parliament. The PJD is not the only Islamist party in the country, but it is extremely popular among the people and has actively sought to curb corruption in the Moroccan government. Human rights organizations in the country have also reported that the government continues to crack down on those who criticize the king. In fact, criticizing the king is illegal under the constitution.

Tunisia's Transition to Democracy

The Arab Spring played out differently in each country that saw protest, and in northern Africa the three countries that experienced revolutions have developed in very different ways in the years since. While Egypt returned to a similar dynamic as it had seen under Mubarak, Tunisia has developed into a stable, democratic country.

Despite some tension between political factions, Tunisia has largely been able to maintain stability and make progress toward reforms since 2011. In 2015, the Nobel Institute recognized the work of the National Dialogue Quartet, a group of four organizations that has exhaustively helped mediate on issues and advocate for democracy in Tunisia. The Quartet, which includes organizations representing laborers, human rights advocates, and lawyers, has been key in easing tension between Islamist, **secular**, and opposition groups within the elected government. While tension still exists, Tunisia has emerged from the Arab Spring as the only state to establish a vibrant democracy and introduce a **liberal** constitution.

But while Tunisia's government has largely maintained stability, unrest in Libya has threatened to spill over into the country, and a terrorist attack at a seaside resort in early 2016 raised concerns about extremism.

Libyan Civil War

Libya, long ruled by dictator Muammar Gaddafi, has splintered into warring groups and states since 2011. The militias that rose up against Gaddafi have begun fighting each other, trying to stake a claim to power in the country.

Tribalism has long been on the decline in Libya as a source of political power, but tribal identity has remained active in much the way someone would identify with his or her home state. When the revolution broke out and violence began, militias born out of tribes began forming primarily in a bid to avoid marginalization—tribes wanted to make sure that their concerns were heard by the government and that they could secure some political power. But in the power vacuum that was left behind after Gaddafi, tensions and rivalries were revived between tribes, particularly among the three former federal provinces Libya had been governed as until 1963. The east and west of the country began vying for authority, effectively splitting Libya in two.

In the east, the Tobruk government, which was elected in 2014 and has been recognized as the Libyan government by world powers, holds sway. From the capital city of Tripoli, however, the Islamist General National Congress, led by the Muslim Brotherhood, controls most of the west. Other groups also exercise power locally, such as the Tuareg militias of Ghat in the southwest or militias in the Misrata district. Most troublingly, the Islamic State (or ISIS) has taken control of the city of Sirte, as well as the surrounding area, giving it a stronghold among the instability. ISIS, which rose out of the Syrian civil war, is an Islamist extremist group that the international community has struggled to confront. Despite a United Nations brokered cease-fire, the factions have not fully disarmed or moved toward centralizing control under the unity government, called the Government of National Accord.

Algeria's Authoritarianism

Abdelaziz Bouteflika has ruled Algeria since 1999, holding power through elections that are believed to be fraudulent.

Following the 1992 to 1999 civil war in Algeria, the government put in place a strong authoritarian government. The military-backed presidential candidate Abdelaziz Bouteflika won the state's first post–civil war presidential election. Although originally pitted against six other candidates, all but Bouteflika left the race shortly before elections were held. This established what would become a pattern of essentially **uncontested** elections that continue to this day. Bouteflika granted immunity to many who participated in the civil war and in early 2011 lifted the state of emergency that had been put in place in 1992.

Algeria's politics are, in many ways, a throwback to pre–Arab Spring governance. Bouteflika's government is still built on authoritarianism, like his former counterparts in Libya, Egypt, and Tunisia. His power is underpinned by a military establishment. Algeria has the largest army on the continent, and high-ranking officials are given a great deal of freedom from the law. Although the multiparty system is allowed to exist, the president's party wins a majority in each election. The country is often referred to as a police state, in which power is maintained through heavy-handed use of police forces and close monitoring of citizens by intelligence services.

Although protests in recent years have revealed the simmering discontent below the surface of Algerian society,

The Tuareg

The Tuareg are a nomadic people who once controlled northern African trade routes. Today, tribes are found in Algeria, Libya, Mali, and Niger, with smaller numbers in Nigeria and Burkina Faso. The Tuareg are often called "the blue people of the Sahara" due to the indigo turbans men of the tribe wear; the indigo can rub off on their skin, leaving a blue mark. Their society is traditionally pastoral, with their economy based on agriculture and livestock as well as trade. Although many are still nomadic, others have settled into semipermanent lifestyles, which has allowed them to expand educational opportunities and develop a more secure economy. Others, particularly young members of the tribe, have moved into cities.

Like other nomadic tribes, the Tuareg have had to adapt to borders put in place after colonial rule ended. Countries often discriminate against nomadic tribes, forcing these populations to change their way of life to better suit modern society. For the Tuareg, thousands found refuge in Muammar Gaddafi's Libya, where they were granted safety but considered second-class citizens. After the revolution of 2011, the Tuareg were once again forced to adapt to changing politics, and since 2013 the tribe has been fighting a fellow nomadic tribe, the Tebu, for control in Libya's southwest.

the country has been able to move from civil war to reliable stability. The country has dedicated great effort to fighting extremism both within its own borders and in neighboring states like Mali, where it assists the United States and other allies to counter jihadist groups.

Regional Relations

Northern Africa has a complex place in African relations, due in large part to the states' close alignment with the Middle East. Egypt, for example, is most often referred to as part of the Middle East rather than northern Africa, underlining its close ties and relations with Middle Eastern states. However, all northern African countries, with the exception of Morocco, are part of the African Union.

Relations between states in northern Africa have been complicated by recent unrest in Libya, Tunisia, and Egypt. Algeria and Morocco have had a closed border—meaning people cannot pass back and forth over the countries' shared border—since 1994, and relations have never thawed between the two countries after the 1963 Sand War over the Western Sahara. The Sawhari Republic has been recognized by Mauritania and Algeria, where the SADR has refugee camps. Yet the Arab Maghreb Union, which was founded to help facilitate trade and economic cooperation among northern African states, has been inactive since 2011.

One of the primary concerns in northern Africa is the rise of extremist groups. Concern that unrest could spill over from unstable countries has driven a rise in tensions between regional states in recent years. This is a particular concern for Egypt and Tunisia, states that established stronger relations after their respective revolutions in 2011 but now have struggled to find a solution to the crisis in Libya.

Algeria's National Liberation Front

Today, the National Liberation Front (or FLN) is the ruling party of Algeria. Led by long-time president Abdelaziz Bouteflika, the group has become the establishment in Algerian politics. But the FLN wasn't always in power. Formed in 1954, the FLN was a revolutionary independence party that fought against French occupation. The group's military wing, the National Liberation Army, or ALN, was responsible for a series of attacks against French sites that sparked the Algerian war for independence. The ALN has been accused of killing thousands of civilians during the conflict and carrying out terrorist attacks in France during the war.

Following independence in 1962, the FLN became the only legal political party under the constitution, but infighting among party leadership made its control unstable. Protests in the late 1980s against one-party rule prompted an amendment to the constitution allowing other political parties to run for office, but in 1990 a coup caused the Algerian civil war, during which time the country was under military rule. Since the war ended in 1999, Algeria has been ruled by Bouteflika. Although other political parties are able to legally exist and run in elections, the FLN remains the most powerful political party in the country. This highlights a key issue in African politics; often, when a party gains control, it holds on to it for as long as possible.

World Relations

Just as regional relations have been complicated by unrest and political change, so have world relations between the international community and northern African states. Some, such as Algeria and Mauritania, have strong strategic relationships with international countries, like the United States, because of the role they have been willing to play in fighting extremism. The Sawhari Republic, meanwhile, has remained a marginal actor (a country excluded from the mainstream with limited political sway) due to the circumstances within the SADR.

In recent years, China has emerged as a significant trade partner with states in northern Africa; in 2012, Egypt, Libya, and Algeria were among the top ten countries receiving Chinese investment. But trade with China has also introduced competition for local markets that has undermined local industry.

As unrest continues in Egypt and Libya, the primary international concern for northern Africa is stemming the tide of refugees that have been migrating to Turkey and Europe. Hundreds of thousands have fled ongoing violence in the region, creating a humanitarian crisis the international community has struggled to contain.

These Nigerian women are attending a health meeting. Health education is crucial in places where care is not always accessible.

2 | Western Africa

Western Africa, which stretches from the Atlantic coast in the west to near the center of the continent along the Gulf of Guinea, is made up of fourteen countries. The north of the region is part of the Sahara Desert, while the south and bulk of the region is coastal and sub-Saharan.

Like other regions in Africa, the country borders that we know today did not exist until colonization. For most of history, the region was dominated by various continental empires, including the fourth-century Ghana Empire and the thirteenth-century Mali Empire. Beyond that, tribal groups oversaw day-to-day affairs and governed relations across western Africa. Many were structured as kingdoms, ruling over broad territories that encompassed many ethnic and cultural groups.

In the late 1880s, European powers began colonizing Africa in what is now known as the Scramble for Africa, referring to the speed with which powers tried to secure control. Western Africa had already been the focus of some European colonization, particularly around ports. By 1913, western Africa was controlled mainly by the French, although there were also German, Portuguese, and British territories. Liberia, which was founded by the American Colonization

Society in the mid-1800s, received independence in 1862 and was not colonized by European powers. Traces of colonialism continue to affect the governance of western Africa. The region is characterized by states with constitutions, yet power struggles can cause unrest.

Colonization

Most states in western Africa came under colonial control during the nineteenth century. Coastal states, like the Gambia, became points of trade for foreign powers, including the Portuguese. By 1900, the French controlled most of the area, with the British holding Sierra Leone, Ghana, and Nigeria. The French held Senegal, Mali, Guinea, Ivory Coast, Burkina Faso, Benin, and Niger. The Portuguese, meanwhile, held Cape Verde (also known as Cabo Verde) and Guinea-Bissau. The only state to maintain independence was Liberia.

The French imposed their own language and educational system in most of their colonies, including those in western Africa. All territory held by the French was governed from Senegal by a governor-general. After the end of World War II, the French government gave limited **autonomy** to its colonies, granting them seats in the French Constituent Assembly and recognizing the countries as part of the French Community rather than an empire. All colonies were granted full independence from France in 1960.

The British also imposed their own culture on native groups, changing the social order and education system. The British also maintained very distinct barriers between classes and races, and like other colonizing powers saw their territories in western Africa as economic opportunities to be exploited. With the fall of the British Empire after World War II, states like Ghana and Nigeria began calling for independence. It came

Porto Novo is the capital of Benin. Benin has experienced coups and political instability since independence from France in 1960.

gradually: in 1957 for Ghana, in 1960 for Nigeria, in 1961 for Sierra Leone, and in 1965 for the Gambia.

The Portuguese had the smallest colonial holding in western Africa, and one of the most unique. Along with Guinea-Bissau, Portugal established a colony on Cape Verde, an **archipelago**, or small set of islands, around 350 miles (563 kilometers) from the African coast. The ten volcanic islands that make up the country were discovered in the fifteenth century and were not inhabited, meaning that when the Portuguese established a colony on the islands there was not an indigenous population. The country became a trading center due to its location along the slave trade routes across the Atlantic. Guinea-Bissau gained independence in 1974 after decades of rebellion, and Cape Verde was granted independence in 1975.

Liberia, however, was never a colony. The country was established by the American Colonization Society, an organization that founded the country as a place for freeborn African Americans. An estimated thirteen thousand people were moved to Liberia from America by 1867. Liberia declared independence as a republic in 1847, but the United States didn't recognize its **sovereignty** until after the civil war, in 1862.

The colonial era, in Africa and around the world, was one marked by inequality and injustice. Colonial powers most often exploited the resources of their colonies and took all profits and products produced by local labor. Local politics were repressed, giving rise to militia and rebel groups that often vied for power after independence, feeding instability. In western Africa, most countries experienced extreme upheaval in the years after independence, including military coups and rebellions. Although this unrest took place for many reasons, the legacy of colonialism and the authoritarian-like rule that came with it bears some of the responsibility.

Government Structures

The governments of western Africa are similarly structured to one another today, although the way politics unfold in each country varies greatly. All states have constitutions that include an elected president and legislature, but some also have a prime minister, appointed by the president and with whom the president shares power.

Presidential elections oftentimes cause turmoil in western Africa, and coups have been common in almost all regional states. Constitutions in most states have been rewritten and amended, often by public referendum, although the frequency with which the military and other outside forces become involved in governance undermines the power of these formal documents.

Political Instability

Very few countries in western Africa were able to smoothly transition from colonialism to independence. With few exceptions, the politics of the second half of the twentieth century were marked by coups, **military juntas**, rebellions, and authoritarian leadership. The political instability has contributed to economic issues and the lack of development in the region, as well as the prevalence of poverty and disease.

Most countries in western Africa experienced several coups, some just years after independence. In Benin, the first president was overthrown in a coup in 1963, and subsequent leaders were also forced out of office. Even a council of three former presidents, known as a triumvirate, was overthrown in a coup. Burkina Faso saw numerous coups throughout the 1970s and 1980s, and attempted coups since then have failed. In the Gambia, Guinea, Guinea-Bissau, Mali, and Nigeria, coups were common for most of the twentieth century.

In Ivory Coast, a 1999 coup triggered a wave of violence and instability that descended into civil war in 2000. Fighting stopped for periods of time throughout the early 2000s, and in 2013 elections were widely boycotted. The instability undermined decades of peace under authoritarian rulers, and the country has yet to recover.

Political instability affects more than just who is in office. A state that is unable to govern effectively is unable to meet the needs of its people, including providing education, opportunity, and health care. Illegal activity can flourish, including exploitation of workers, as occurs in the diamond industry of Sierra Leone. In some countries, slavery is still practiced despite being illegal. In Guinea, political instability has undermined the state's health care system and left many people in poverty, and as a result the country was the epicenter of the 2013 Ebola epidemic that swept across the region.

Diamond miners in Sierra Leone often work in unsafe conditions.

Instability also provides opportunities for non-state actors (groups that are not part of the formal political structure but still wield considerable influence in a state's affairs) or terrorist groups to gain influence, as we've seen in Nigeria. The government has been ineffective in containing and confronting extremist group Boko Haram, an ISIS-affiliated Islamist group that has carried out attacks in neighboring countries. The group has also routinely kidnapped girls and women, who are forced to marry fighters, and has massacred entire communities.

But not all states in western Africa have experienced coups and instability. Cape Verde is one of the most stable and democratic countries in the world, ranked thirty-first by the Democracy Index. Senegal has also seen several peaceful transitions of power and has never experienced a coup. Both countries rank highly on the Ibrahim Index, a measure of governance in African countries.

Military Rule

Along with coups, for many western African countries military rule has been imposed at various times in the twentieth and twenty-first centuries. Military rule is exactly what it sounds like; the military or armed forces take control of a country's government. Oftentimes this is accompanied by **martial law**, in which the constitution and other governing bodies are dissolved. States can also become police states, in which the population is monitored and order is maintained through the heavy presence of military or police forces.

In Togo, Sierra Leone, Niger, Burkina Faso, Ghana, and Guinea, the military assumed control of the country at various points. In other countries, including Benin and Liberia, the military was involved in coups that unseated leaders, both elected and authoritarian.

Military rule is a complex phenomenon. Although there's an immediate negative reaction when the military overtakes civilian rule (and often rightly so given the track record military juntas have of unjust rule), the military is sometimes able to effectively restore order and stability.

Sometimes, in dire circumstances, the decision between order and instability is one that can mean the difference between life and death. If a state is unstable and unable to govern for too long, it can give rise to numerous issues, including public health concerns, humanitarian crises, and the rise of terrorist groups. But military rule, by its nature authoritarian, can make it easier to direct resources where needed and to confront threats immediately.

Development

States in western Africa are among the least developed in the world, which is due in part to political instability and civil conflict. A developing country, which is how most states in western Africa are defined, refers to a poor country with an economy often built on agriculture. Developing countries often experience high poverty, inequality, and political instability, and they rank low on human rights indicators. These states often rely on international aid or humanitarian assistance, and for some the United Nations provides peacekeepers and special missions to aid in development.

Of the forty-eight countries considered least developed by the United Nations Committee for Development Policy, eleven are in western Africa. Only Cape Verde, Ghana, Nigeria, and Ivory Coast are left off the list. According to the Human Development Index, which ranks countries based on factors such as literacy and life expectancy, Niger is the least developed country in the world, with Burkina Faso, Guinea, Sierra Leone, Mali, and Guinea-Bissau in the bottom ten. Western African countries make up almost half of the bottom twenty.

Lack of development has serious consequences for the politics of western Africa. In underdeveloped countries, low literacy makes it difficult for a political culture to exist among the public, and it makes it much easier for the government to manipulate information. This serves the desires of authoritarian rulers, making it easier for them to hold on to power. But it makes it difficult for states to transition to democracy and foster vibrant political and civil society. Underdevelopment also leads to poverty, which in some cases can cause tension and violence between groups that see each other as competition for limited resources. In impoverished countries, women are often excluded from the economy, and in many cases they are also excluded from politics or education.

Overcoming underdevelopment can be difficult in and of itself, and that difficulty is increased significantly when coupled with issues like a legacy of civil war. In Liberia, one of the world's least developed countries, this struggle is being seen as President Ellen Johnson Sirleaf works to move her country forward. Sirleaf is the first female president of an African country and was elected shortly after the Second Liberian Civil War ended. She has been working to reconcile the country and hold those responsible for the violence accountable.

Faced with a legacy of violence, corruption, and authoritarianism, as well as complications caused by poverty and disease, Sirleaf has taken on the daunting task of bringing the country back from the edge of collapse. Yet her critics are worried that she has not done enough to remedy the many problems facing the country, highlighting the slow and difficult road of governing.

Human Rights

Politics do not take place in a vacuum, something that is extremely clear in the case of underdeveloped or developing countries. Governments that aren't able to govern are unable to meet the needs of their people, direct resources where needed, and confront illegal practices, such as illegal deforestation or toxic waste dumping in the water supply. In some cases, the government itself is responsible for human rights abuses, as in the Gambia where President Yahya Jammeh, an unpredictable leader, had hundreds arrested on suspicion of witchcraft after his aunt became ill.

In western Africa, human rights abuses have been recorded across the region, and civil wars have created humanitarian crises. In Sierra Leone, a violent, decade-long civil war not only killed many but has left hundreds of thousands with long-term post-traumatic mental health issues, including the many children forced to fight by rebel groups. In 2003, former Liberian president Charles Taylor was

Gorée Island

In the fifteenth through seventeenth centuries, the majority of slaves taken to the New World were from western Africa. The Atlantic slave trade was established by the Europeans, including the Portuguese, British, and Spanish. An exact number of people taken from Africa as slaves is not known, but estimates range from ten to twenty-eight million. Far fewer survived passage across the Atlantic.

On Gorée Island, the House of Slaves was built in 1776 to imprison men, women, and children before their voyage across the Atlantic. It was converted into a memorial and museum in 1962. The museum includes the basement cells in which slaves were held prior to boarding ships, and the haunting Door of No Return has become a place of reflection for tourists and world leaders. The door, which overlooks the Atlantic, would have been the captives' route onto the ships and the area around it the last they would see of Africa. Conditions on the island were horrific, with large numbers of people held in small areas with no ventilation. Those who died were thrown into the ocean, and sexual violence against female slaves was common. Although there is disagreement among scholars about how many passed through Gorée Island, some estimate more than one million.

accused by a Sierra Leone court of war crimes, crimes against humanity, and violations of international humanitarian law during conflict with the country. These charges include sexual violence, use of child soldiers, and extermination of civilians.

In Togo, Ivory Coast, the Gambia, and Nigeria, human rights violations have been numerous. Countries across the region, including Sierra Leone, Mali, and Guinea, have high rates of forced labor, female circumcision, and discrimination. Slavery, though illegal, is still practiced in Ghana, Togo, Benin, Mali, and Niger.

Politically, the government can limit the people's rights in many ways. Many states are or were at one time one-party states, meaning there was only one legally recognized political party able to take part in elections. This effectively allows one party to control the entire government and takes away the people's right to choose their leaders. In other cases, authoritarian leaders have twisted or rewritten the constitution so that they could legitimize their power and hold on to office, as we've seen in states like Guinea and Ivory Coast.

The government, even when not directly responsible for atrocities and human rights violations, must assume some of the blame. By not acting against contemporary slavery or to ensure the safety of women and children, the state is indirectly responsible for widespread practices that violate human rights. Such inaction or continued political repression can lead to uprisings, coups, rebellions and other armed conflict aimed at regime change, which can destabilize a country significantly, as happened in Ivory Coast.

Non-State Actors in Western Africa

Terrorism across the continent is beyond the scope of this book, but it is important to note that for western Africa, non-state actors and terrorist organizations have posed significant problems for governments. The region has seen an increase in extremist activity in recent years, including attacks against civilians in Niger and Burkina Faso.

"Non-state actors" can refer to several kinds of groups, and in western Africa groups like the Tuareg fit the bill as they have engaged in rebellions with frequency. A non-state actor is not necessarily a terrorist organization, but there is significant overlap, including in western Africa.

Two of the largest groups in western Africa are al-Qaeda in the Islamic Maghreb (or AQIM) and Boko Haram. Boko Haram is active primarily in Nigeria, where it carries out attacks against villages and the government regularly. The group rose to international prominence in 2014 when they kidnapped hundreds of schoolgirls from the village of Chibok. ISIS is also active in the region, having a foothold in the largely unstable Libya, and the AQIM splinter group Movement for Unity and Jihad in West Africa has a limited presence.

These groups not only undermine security but also challenge central authority through violence. Non-state actors thrive in countries where instability allows them to control broad stretches of territory, such as northern Mali. They also give authoritarian rulers a **scapegoat** for crackdowns against dissidents and the press, as governments are able to cite security concerns to do so. These groups often target civilians, creating a climate of fear and disrupting the economy. In this way, these groups also threaten development and continue the cycle of violence and poverty that created the conditions for their rise in the first place, while also keeping the government's limited resources directed away from public programs that would help the people.

Regional Relations

All states in western Africa are members of the Economic Community for West African States (ECOWAS), an organization set up to help facilitate economic cooperation in the region. In 1990, the organization also developed a nonaggression protocol and mutual defense agreement for member states, as instability and regional conflict have greatly shaped relations in western Africa.

Charles Taylor, once the president of Liberia, was accused of crimes against humanity following the Liberian Civil War.

Many states have experienced border clashes and some have become involved in conflicts in other countries. The Second Liberian Civil War was funded in part by Liberia's president Charles Taylor, who used money from the Sierra Leone's diamond industry to supply rebels with arms and weapons. Benin and Burkina Faso have long disputed their mutual claim to Koualou village on their shared border, and similar conflicts have arisen between Ivory Coast and Guinea, as well as Benin and Nigeria.

Ongoing conflict in the region has also caused a refugee crisis. Violence has forced hundreds of thousands from their homes in Togo, Ivory Coast, Liberia, and Sierra Leone. Mali, where extremist groups such as al-Qaeda have begun claiming villages, also faces a refugee crisis. In Nigeria, the threat from Boko Haram has forced many to leave their homes as well. This has put considerable strain on the already

Niger Delta Militants

Non-state actors pose substantial threats to governance in western Africa, and militant groups have targeted many of the countries in the region. In Nigeria, a new group was announced in early 2016, taking the name of Niger Delta Avengers. The group was formed in the poor Niger Delta and targets the country's oil industry, a key source of income for the government. It is not the first such group to come out of the region; in 2009, the government granted amnesty to several so-called oil militancy groups that demanded greater financial assistance for those who live in the oil-rich area and suffer from poverty as well as environmental degradation caused by oil production.

The Niger Delta Avengers are believed to be led by a guerrilla named Government Ekpemupolo (he is also referred to by the alias Tompolo). The group has carried out almost daily attacks against the oil industry, cutting production significantly. In February 2016, the group shut down a terminal that produces 250,000 barrels of oil per day by blowing up a pipeline. Such attacks have pushed international companies to back out of their contractual agreements with the country, further threatening the Nigerian economy. Former militants are encouraging the group to negotiate a peace with the government, but so far the Niger Delta Avengers have refused such offers.

struggling economies of states like the Gambia, Benin, and Guinea. The United Nations and other organizations have been extremely active in the region, assisting in both the care of refugees and implementing plans to help them return to their home countries.

Some countries in the region have struggled to maintain stability due to Tuareg rebels. In Mali and Niger, the Tuareg have risen up multiple times against the government due to lack of representation and marginalization. In Mali, violence has led to the declaration of states of emergency and martial law, and in both Mali and Niger, peace talks have failed to build a lasting agreement. Both countries have worked together in the past to contain the fighting, but with the rise of al-Qaeda and more recently, the Macina Liberation Front in Mali, instability has gone beyond the Tuareg.

World Relations

Relations between western Africa and the rest of the international community are largely shaped by the many issues facing the region. Global involvement in development, the spread of deadly diseases such as Ebola, the fight against Boko Haram, negotiating peace, and trying to end drug and human trafficking in the region means that many international groups are active there. The United Nations has numerous missions present in western Africa, and groups like Amnesty International and Human Rights Watch are active. These groups have their own complicated relationships with governments across western Africa.

Bangui, the capital of the Central African Republic, has seen fighting and unrest since civil war began in 2012.

3 Central Africa

C entral Africa is a wide territory located along the Atlantic to the west and bordering eastern and southern Africa on land. According to the African Union, the region includes Burundi, Cameroon, Central African Republic, Chad, Congo, Democratic Republic of Congo, Equatorial Guinea, Gabon, and São Tomé and Príncipe. All states are members of the Economic Community of Central African States and the African Union.

Prior to colonization, central Africa was home to many empires and tribal kingdoms, including the Lunda Empire and the Congo Empire. After independence in the 1960s and 1970s, most countries in central Africa struggled with political instability, dictatorship, and eventually civil war. The region was torn apart by the Congo Civil Wars of the 1990s, and today the Central African Republic civil war is one of the worst humanitarian disasters in the world. The area also struggles with poverty, underdevelopment, and a history of violent conflict.

Colonization

Although eventually most of central Africa was held by France, Germany held some countries until the end of

World War I. Cameroon and part of modern Congo were among the territories that became French colonies, with part of Cameroon controlled by the British. Equatorial Guinea was a Spanish colony, and Burundi was a colony of Belgium. The Portuguese established São Tomé and Príncipe on an uninhabited archipelago, much like Cape Verde.

Chad, the Central African Republic, Congo, the Democratic Republic of Congo, Gabon, and French-controlled Cameroon all became independent in 1960, with British-held Cameroon granted independence the next year. Equatorial Guinea remained a colony until 1968, and São Tomé and Príncipe were granted independence in 1975.

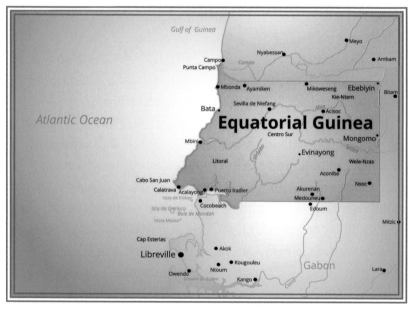

Equatorial Guinea, shown on this map, remained a Spanish colony until 1968.

As in other parts of the world, colonization was a traumatic experience that has had lasting impact on the region's political culture. Central Africa is extremely diverse, with more than seventy languages spoken in the Central

African Republic and more than two hundred in Cameroon alone. In many cases, the colonizing powers used this diversity to their advantage by allowing tension to thrive and then undermining centuries-old structures of governance. In Burundi, as well as in neighboring Rwanda, the colonial administration encouraged rivalry between the ethnic groups the Tutsi and the Hutu. In both Burundi and Rwanda, postcolonialism was marked with political instability and eventual ethnic cleansing and genocide. By pitting rival tribal and ethnic groups against one another, colonial forces were able to ensure their own power was not challenged by keeping the local populations in conflict with one another.

Political Structure

Most countries in central Africa have constitutions that establish democratic republics, with a president and in some cases a prime minister. Each country has a legislature that is elected by popular vote, as is the president. But most countries have rewritten and amended their constitutions many times, and in some cases the government functions more as an authoritarian state. In Equatorial Guinea, for example, President Teodoro Obiang is the longest-serving dictator in Africa, holding office from 1979 to today.

Even in states with democratic elections, such as São Tomé and Príncipe, the president holds a great deal of power. In Gabon, which instituted considerable reforms in the 1990s, the president remains the power center of the country. In most states, a history of coups and regime change has left the political structure weak. Many governments, including in Burundi, Cameroon, and the Central African Republic, struggle to claim legitimacy in the face of marginalization, continued violence, and ethnic tension.

Teodoro Obiang

As president of Equatorial Guinea, Teodoro Obiang Nguema Mbasogo, known as Teodoro Obiang, holds the title of Africa's longest-serving dictator. He is also the longest-serving president in the world, although the title obscures his true role in politics. He first came to power in 1979, when a military coup unseated his uncle, who was the country's first postindependence president. Soon after taking office, he began reversing his uncle's repression by opening houses of worship and freeing political prisoners. Although these early actions suggested that he would be more humane than his uncle, since then Equatorial Guinea has become a one-party state under Obiang's Democratic Party of Equatorial Guinea. International organizations have expressed concern about the country's high corruption and ethnic discrimination. The constitution allows Obiang to "rule by decree," meaning he can make laws without the legislature's approval. His government also runs Black Beach Prison, a notorious prison in the capital where torture is believed to be carried out against prisoners.

Obiang's government does not allow dissent, and as a result all opposition groups have had to work in exile. This includes EG Justice, the first international organization for human rights in Equatorial Guinea. It is led by Tutu Alicante, an Equatorial Guinean who left his country at the age of nineteen to pursue a career in human rights law and activism. Alicante has become one of the leading voices against Obiang's repressive state, and he works to spread awareness of the government's human rights record.

Political Instability

For most of the twentieth century, central Africa was beset by political instability. Multiple countries experienced civil wars, with Burundi experiencing two during the 1970s and 1990s. Others, such as Congo, spent great periods of time as one-party states, with no opposition taking root.

In some cases, however, stability has been able to be restored, even if it has meant authoritarian rulers taking control of the country. Cameroon, for example, has been led by President Paul Biya since 1984, but the stability in the country has allowed industry to flourish. Similarly, Gabon experienced frequent coups until a new constitution and reforms were approved in 1990. Since then the country has become one of the most prosperous in the region, despite the considerable power retained by the president and poor income distribution, leaving much of the country in poverty.

The exception, much like in western Africa, is the island country established by Portugal. São Tomé and Príncipe has experienced unrest, and several coup attempts have been thwarted while others took place with little impact on governance. Once a one-party state, it has been able to embrace political pluralism peacefully. Today, the country is

São Tomé and Príncipe have become resort destinations due to their political stability and beautiful natural landscape.

impoverished but stable, ranking eleventh on the Ibrahim Index of African Governance.

Several countries in the region have experienced uprisings, rebellions, or other calls for greater autonomy. In the Democratic Republic of Congo, rebel groups in the east were able to gain control of enough territory to eventually join Rwanda in waging war against the government twice, discussed in greater detail below. A war between rebels and government forces also took place in the Central African Republic from 2004 to 2007.

In Cameroon, where the British and French split the territory between them, unrest has been common as the English-speaking regions demand equality. Some have begun agitating for an independent state in the southwest. Cameroon is predominantly a French-speaking country, and the government is run entirely by French speakers. English speakers are barred from holding top offices, and all government documents are published only in French. The government has clashed repeatedly in recent years with English-speaking rebels and protesters.

Congo Civil Wars

In the 1990s and early 2000s, two regional conflicts destabilized the region and left millions dead. The conflicts are called the Congo Civil Wars because they took place in the Democratic Republic of Congo, or Zaire as it was called until after the First Congo War. The first took place from 1996 to 1997, and the second from 1998 to 2003. The Second Congo War is the deadliest since World War II, causing an estimated 5.4 million deaths from fighting, starvation, and disease.

The First Congo War began in 1997, when then-Zaire was invaded by Rwanda. The nation had been under the control of dictator Mobutu Sese Seko since

Congolese soldiers take part in a training exercise near Kisangani.

independence thirty-seven years earlier. Under Mobutu,
Zaire had experienced economic decline and widespread
corruption. Rebel groups, including leftists and ethnic groups
marginalized by the capital, operated with some freedom
in the east along the border with Rwanda. Following the
Rwandan Genocide in 1994, Hutu *génocidaires*, or those
responsible for the mass killings, took refuge in eastern Zaire.
In 1995, Rwandan Tutsi militias began carrying out attacks
against the Hutus in Zaire, sparking an uprising. Rwanda
supported the Alliance Democratic Forces for the Liberation
of Congo (ADFL), which transformed the unrest into an
antigovernment movement.

Rwandan defense minister Paul Kagame claimed that
plans had been found outlining a Zairian invasion of Rwanda.
This justified Rwanda's calls for Mobutu to be overthrown.
Uganda worked closely with Rwanda in the conflict, sending
soldiers to Zaire and assisting in planning. Angola entered the

conflict in 1997, also joining forces against Mobutu. Other states, such as Burundi, had a limited role in supporting Rwanda, while Zaire hired mercenaries and received support from Sudan. Rwandan forces succeeded in forcing Mobutu into exile, but tension remained after ADFL leader Laurent-Desire Kabila took over the presidency, setting the stage for the Second Congo War.

The Second Congo War began for many of the same reasons as the first did, including the presence of armed Hutu rebels in poorly controlled east Zaire, by then renamed the Democratic Republic of Congo. At its height, the Second Congo War involved nine different countries, including Sudan, Chad, Libya, Angola, Uganda, Tanzania, and Zimbabwe, among others. It stretched from the north of Africa to the southern tip, with South Africa aligned politically with the Democratic Republic of Congo. Armed militia groups also flourished.

Millions were displaced during the six years of fighting, with numerous cease-fires broken and violence resurging multiple times. The conflict had lasting effects, including limited medical aid and food shortages. In 2004, an estimated one thousand people died each day from malnutrition and disease. According to the International Rescue Committee, a total of 5.4 million were killed before the war ended.

In 2006, the Democratic Republic of Congo seemed like it was making progress. The nation held a multiparty presidential election that year. Yet the **incumbent** president, Joseph Kabila, was reelected to office, and uprisings in rebel-held areas continued. Armed groups remain active in parts of the Democratic Republic of Congo, and the country has struggled to overcome the legacy of violence left behind by the wars. The use of sexual violence and child soldiers

Rebels, like those pictured here, control much of CAR's border areas and continue to fight with CAR's military.

remains common, and warlords reign in disputed areas across the country using extreme violence against the population.

The crisis in the Democratic Republic of Congo is one created in part by a lack of rule, rather than aggression by the government. Poor central control has allowed armed groups to take control of areas and unleash a reign of terror on the country, brutalizing citizens with campaigns of unimaginable violence. The government of the Democratic Republic of Congo is unable to respond adequately, and so the situation continues to deteriorate.

Central African Republic Civil War

In late 2012, fighting broke out between the government in the Central African Republic, or CAR, and a coalition of armed Muslim groups called the Seleka. The Seleka captured the capital in March of the following year, staging a coup shortly thereafter. In response, Christian militias known as "anti-balaka" groups began taking up arms against the Muslim rebels, beginning an ongoing conflict that has torn CAR apart and destabilized the country.

The conflict in CAR is largely defined by **sectarianism**. Muslims and Christians have been reportedly carrying out attacks against civilians on the basis of faith. The United Nations and other human rights groups have reported that the violence amounts to war crimes and crimes against humanity, including mass genocide and sexual violence.

The Central African Republic, like the Democratic Republic of Congo, is extremely rich in resources and fertile land. But the ongoing conflict both countries have experienced has drastically impacted the country's politics and development. CAR is one of the ten poorest countries in the world and ranks second to last on the Human Development Index. Since the start of fighting, an estimated six thousand have been killed and seven hundred thousand, or one-fifth of the population, have been displaced. Sixty percent of the population lives in poverty, and more than two million people are believed to be in immediate need of assistance.

A new president, Faustin-Archange Touadera, was inaugurated in March 2016. Although he is supported by much of the public and CAR's violence has slowed, the reasons for the conflict still exist. Armed groups still hold broad territories, and they have the ability to motivate fighters by encouraging tension. Years of war have also caused young people to grow up in conflict, and in general, they are less educated than their parents.

CAR illustrates the importance of a unifying **national identity** to maintaining peace. National identity does not replace other core personal values, such as religion or heritage. It also doesn't guarantee conflict won't take place. But it does provide a central set of values and sense of cohesion that can lessen perceived differences and tension due to diversity.

Development

Development is an important topic when discussing Africa. The infrastructure of a country sheds light on that nation's politics and governance. The level of a nation's development can be the direct result of governance—or even inspire regime change.

Of the countries in central Africa, just Gabon and Congo are not on the list of least developed countries in the world. CAR ranks 187th out of 188, with Chad at 185, Burundi at 184, the Democratic Republic of Congo at 176, and Cameroon at 153. São Tomé and Príncipe ranks just above the low development line at 143.

Development is measured using data most often collected by countries themselves. This can include economic data or birth, death, and literacy rates. These are also the statistics on which international development programs exist, including those conducted by the United Nations and international aid packages.

But for central Africa, using these measures isn't straightforward. Most countries in the region struggle to gather the necessary data to provide a comprehensive picture of the situation on the ground. This is due to many factors. One is conflict; it's nearly impossible for a state to gather accurate data in a warzone or in a region where the regular institutions that would gather the data are no longer stable, such as hospitals and schools. Another is governments using bad data; national accounting figures have been found to be off by as much as half in past research, and playing with the numbers can get a government extra funding. When the United Nations or other organizations step in to gather data, they often use old or partial information out of necessity— sometimes there's simply nothing else available.

In extreme cases, such as CAR, observers can see for themselves the desperate needs of the people. But judging progress as countries recover from conflict or begin growing is more difficult, although at that point it is just as crucial. International organizations such as the World Bank have committed funding and made proposals to revitalize data gathering in the region, committing as much as $11.28 per person in CAR. More nongovernment organizations, such as Code for Africa, are also working to help gather and publish data.

Human Rights

The human rights record in central Africa is marked by war crimes, crimes against humanity, and other repression and violence. Almost every country has experienced unrest that has led to extreme violence against civilians, with the Democratic Republic of Congo and the Central African Republic as the best-known cases. Yet those two countries aren't alone, and sadly the norm across the region and with few exceptions is routine political violence, sexual violence, and corruption.

Chad, which experienced a civil war just five years after gaining independence from France in 1960, is one of the poorest and most corrupt countries in the world. When the Darfur crisis broke out in nearby Sudan, the country saw a huge number of refugees cross the border, which has destabilized the already weak country. The former president of Chad, Hissene Habre, has been charged with crimes against humanity, war crimes, and torture, and he has been accused of ordering thousands of political killings. He went on trial in Senegal in May 2016.

Slavery is still common in Congo and the Democratic Republic of Congo, where slaves are forced to work in gold mines. In the Congo, much of the ethnic minority Pygmy population is born into slavery, forced to serve the majority Bantu population. Violent punishment, sexual violence, and discrimination have been observed by human rights groups, but the government has shown no desire to protect the Pygmy population.

Prior to colonization, Bantus and Pygmies lived in peace. The Pygmies are traditionally nomadic jungle inhabitants, while the Bantu established stable villages. The two groups interacted loosely, with the Pygmies trading in town before returning to the jungle. That changed with the introduction of the colonial power structure. Under the French, the Bantu were treated like slaves. Today, they carry out the same treatment on the Pygmies.

This phenomenon is common in some postcolonial states, in which one group takes power and uses it in much the same way colonial forces did. In other cases, ethnic discrimination established or strengthened under colonial rule has lived on in politics today. In Burundi and Rwanda, discussed in the following chapter in greater detail, the Tutsis and the Hutus were defined primarily by their economic means prior to Belgium colonizing the countries. The two groups, though originally ethnically separate, had formed one group, with their distinct names signaling economic status and power rather than ethnic differences. Yet the Belgians enforced the idea that these two groups were truly distinct by making them carry identity cards and by favoring the Tutsis, who were able to go to school and take positions of power.

African Nationalism

African Nationalism was one of the defining movements of the late nineteenth century, a driving force in the fight against colonization, and the basis for groups like the African Union today. African Nationalism emerged in the late 1800s and is built on the idea of African unity and self-rule. It is believed to have been introduced by Edward Wilmot Blyden, a Liberian writer and politician who advocated for Africans (and those of African descent) to work toward improving the continent. His writings became the basis for political organizations and parties as early as the 1890s. Parties, militias, and organizations born out of African Nationalism went on to fight against colonizing forces, playing a key role in securing independence for the continent.

After independence, African Nationalism continued to be influential. Now known as Pan-Africanism, African Nationalism led to the formation of groups like the Organization for African Unity, today called the African Union. Although African Nationalism/Pan-Africanism respects the independence of all African states, it supports cooperation and close relations between states to help build African economies, culture, and politics. Pan-African groups, such as the Pan-Africanist Congress in South Africa, have been involved in the political evolution of the continent and take on issues ranging from globalization to the environment to human rights concerns. They also work to spread an awareness of Africa's shared culture, both across the continent and into the **diaspora**.

Edward Wilmot Blyden was the father of African Nationalism, a driving ideology behind independence movements in the twentieth century.

This policy led to genocide in both Rwanda and Burundi, and the tension between the two groups continues to flare into violence today. In Burundi, the Tutsi-controlled military and government carried out mass killings of the Hutu in 1972. In 1993, the Hutu population carried out similar mass killings of Tutsis. Both of these events have been called genocide by the United Nations and have been labeled ethnic cleansing, or an attempt to kill out an entire ethnic group.

Other political violations of human rights, such as discrimination against and persecution of minorities, the arrest and torture of opposition leaders, and the effects of corruption in government are common. Much of the population of central Africa lives in poverty or survives through subsistence farming, meaning they are able to grow just enough to live. In Equatorial Guinea, most of the country does not have access to clean water, and the infant death rate is high. The continued presence of warlords and rebel forces across the region makes it difficult to ensure the safety of the public.

Regional Relations

Most states in central Africa have functioning relations, but ongoing conflict has broken down many governments' ability to control their own borders. Unsecured borders have allowed rebel groups to move between states with little to no trouble. There are some land disputes in the region, including between Gabon and Equatorial Guinea, Congo and the Democratic Republic of Congo, and Cameroon and Equatorial Guinea. With the exception of the Congo Civil Wars, most conflicts have been internal, including civil wars in Chad and the Central African Republic.

World Relations

Central Africa's world relations have been dominated by the need for trade and peacekeeping efforts. International organizations are very active in the region, and foreign governments provide a great deal of aid to countries like the Central African Republic. Some countries, such as France, have also sent troops to aid in monitoring borders or patrolling zones of unrest. Corruption in many countries means that aid does not necessarily go where it needs to, and the lack of data available about progress makes it difficult to effectively measure the impact of efforts in the region.

Diamonds and gold are mined in several regional countries, but their production is extremely controversial internationally. In countries like the Central African Republic and Congo, mining is done by slaves or forced labor, and miners are often extremely poorly compensated for their dangerous work. What's more, governments often use the money gained from the **precious metals** trade to finance conflict, much as it does in Sierra Leone in western Africa.

Jomo Kenyatta was the first postindependence president of Kenya, and he remains a significant national figure.

JAMES BL

4 | Eastern Africa

astern Africa, bordered by the Indian Ocean, is made up of fourteen countries. Djibouti, Eritrea, Ethiopia, Kenya, Rwanda, Somalia, Sudan, South Sudan, Uganda, and Tanzania are on the mainland of Africa. Comoros, Madagascar, Mauritius, and Seychelles are island nations in the Indian Ocean.

Eastern Africa is **linguistically**, religiously, and culturally diverse. Some states, like Sudan, straddle Africa and the Middle East, while island nations like Mauritius are found in the Indian Ocean. In Kenya, a large Indian influence has contributed to a number of shared cuisines. Eastern Africa is also home to the world's youngest country, South Sudan, which has fallen into ongoing conflict since gaining independence via referendum in 2011.

Eastern Africa has a history of political violence and unrest, including several civil wars and disputes between countries. The region is home to some of the poorest and most corrupt states in the world, as well as some of the most democratic in Africa. Ethnic violence is a significant issue in eastern Africa, and the Rwandan Genocide of 1994 is one of the greatest tragedies in recent history, killing a still unknown number of civilians. In Uganda, the Lord's Resistance Army poses considerable threats to the local population, and the government has failed to curtail the ongoing violence perpetrated by its leader, Joseph Kony. Similarly, Islamist extremist group al-Shabaab is active the region.

German soldiers during the East Africa Campaign, a set of battles fought during World War II between German and British forces

Colonization

Most of eastern Africa was colonized by the British, with a few exceptions. The French held Mauritius, Madagascar, Djibouti, and Comoros, while Belgium ruled Rwanda and Burundi together. Britain and Italy controlled Somalia as two separate states that unified to form the modern state in 1960. Egypt and Britain shared control of Sudan, although Britain maintained primary influence.

Unlike other regions where independence was granted around the same time for most countries, eastern African states were granted independence at various points after 1955. Madagascar was granted independence in 1960, with Uganda gaining independence in 1962 and Rwanda gaining independence in 1963. Tanzania became sovereign in 1964, and Mauritius did so in 1968. Sudan became independent in 1966. Somalia was unified in 1960 but was not independent until 1969. Kenya was a colony until 1963. Some states didn't gain independence until the late 1970s. Comoros became sovereign in 1975, Seychelles in 1976, and Djibouti in 1977.

Eritrea and Ethiopia are unique. Eritrea, a British colony, joined a federation with Ethiopia rather than become independent in 1947, but Ethiopia **annexed** the country. Eritrea became independent of Ethiopia in 1993, following the Eritrean War of Independence. It was the last in the region to gain independence.

Ethiopia, on the other hand, was never a colony. It was the only African country able to resist European forces during the Scramble for Africa of the late 1800s. (Although Liberia was also never a colony, the country did not have to fight against colonizing forces.) Yet maintaining independence did not spare it from later hardship, as will be discussed in the next section.

Government Structures

With the exception of Ethiopia, which is governed by a prime minister, all states in eastern Africa are presidential republics. Countries in the region exist at extreme ends of the political spectrum. In some, such as Kenya and Mauritius, unrest has given rise to largely democratic states, while in others, such as Rwanda and Sudan, politics is dominated by single parties and plagued with corruption.

Djibouti, which experienced extensive armed conflict in the 1990s, resolved fighting through a power-sharing arrangement with the dominant ruling party and the leading political opposition, allowing the state to stabilize. Eritrea, on the other hand, has never held elections, and the state has

instead been ruled by one ruler since independence from
Ethiopia in 1993. In Madagascar, power is consolidated
tightly in the hands of the president and his appointed
prime minister, and political transitions have been marked
by unrest, protests, and coups. This instability has had a
significant impact on the economy, the country's international
relations, and living standards.

Comoros, a small archipelago between the island nation
of Madagascar and the mainland, is one of the most stable
democracies in the region and one of few legitimate electoral
democracies in the Arab world according to Freedom House,
an independent organization that evaluates governments
around the world. The country is ranked fourteenth on the
Ibrahim Index of African Governance. The three major
islands that make up the country are granted local autonomy,
and the presidency passes from island to island each election
cycle. However, the country is also one of the poorest in the
region, with some of the worst income inequality in the world
and very low human development.

Political Instability

Eastern African states have struggled with instability
throughout the postcolonial years of the twentieth century,
including those that are today considered stable. Comoros,
today a democratic country, had around twenty coups or
attempted coups before establishing stability. A coup in 1977
transformed Seychelles from a stable tourist destination to a
one-party state plagued with unrest until 1993.

Tanzania, Uganda, Rwanda, and Eritrea are each
dominated by one party, and Ethiopia is considered an
authoritarian country despite having a multiparty political
system according to the constitution. Kenya was able to

peacefully transition from a dictatorship under Daniel Moi, who ruled the country from 1978 to 2002, to a multiparty democracy. However, the country has seen extreme violence in recent elections, including protests in 2007 that left one thousand dead and displaced six hundred thousand due to ethnically targeted violence. A new constitution in 2010 decentralized some governmental duties, giving local officials more power and providing a bill of rights for citizens.

Many states in eastern Africa have not been able to overcome instability to establish democratic states or a functioning political culture. A coup in Sudan brought to power Omar al-Bashir, a dictator who has imposed a harsh interpretation of Islamic law and is wanted by the International Criminal Court (ICC) on charges of crimes against humanity. He has been in power since 1989 and announced in 2016 that he would step down in 2020.

Eastern Africa also has three fragile or failed states: Somalia, Sudan, and South Sudan. A failed state is defined as a country with a government so weak that it is unable to govern or exert any effective control. The annual Fragile State Index, formerly called the Failed State Index, is compiled by the Fund for Peace, using statistics on migration, public services, poverty, and human rights.

Somalia was put on the list of extremely fragile or failed states in 1991, when the government collapsed and a civil war broke out as groups fought to fill the power vacuum the authoritarian Mohamed Siad Barre left behind. The country was at the top of the list, meaning it was the most unstable and ungoverned state in the world, in both 2008 and 2013. Since 2012, the establishment of a fledgling federal government has allowed the country to begin reestablishing stability. In 2015, it was second on the list of fragile states.

The first spot now belongs to South Sudan, the world's youngest country. It became independent from Sudan in 2011 and has since struggled to maintain order and peace. A split between President Salva Kirr Mayardit and Vice President Riek Machar erupted into a civil war in 2013. Although a unity government was established in 2014, the country remains the least governed in the world. Sudan is number four on the list.

Development

Most of eastern Africa remains underdeveloped, due in no small part to ongoing conflict and political instability. Eleven of the region's fourteen states are on the list of least developed countries, including Comoros. Although stable, Comoros remains extremely impoverished, with 80 percent of the country's budget funding just the electoral system. It is a stark reminder that stability and prosperity do not necessarily walk hand in hand. Seychelles, Mauritius, and Kenya are the only countries in the region that are not considered least developed.

The majority of states in the region are also ranked low on the Human Development Index. Somalia is not on the index at all, due to a lack of data. Seychelles and Mauritius are high on the index, ranking 64 and 63 respectively. Despite some upheaval and protests in recent decades, Mauritius has established itself as an extremely stable country with a strong economy. The World Bank classifies it as an upper-middle-income economy, and Freedom House considers it a free country.

Political Freedom and Human Rights

Political freedom has been restricted across the region at numerous times in recent history. Most countries have experienced at least a brief period of one-state rule, during

Child soldiers, like this Zairian photographed in 1996, have been used by rebel groups and governments in conflicts across Africa.

which elections, if held, were for show rather than true democratic expression. In some cases, a lack of political freedom has been accompanied by political stability; in Rwanda, a strong central one-party government has helped society overcome one of the worst genocides in modern history. In contrast, Madagascar has seen democratic

Somaliland

Somaliland is a separatist region in northern Somalia that declared independence in 1991 but has yet to be recognized by any country or international organization. The region was once a British protectorate, known as British Somaliland. An estimated 3.5 million people live in the area, and the majority religion is Islam. Under the military dictatorship of Mohamed Siad Barre, rebels in the region clashed with government forces. Tens of thousands were killed in the conflict. After the military coup of 1991 unseated Siad Barre, the region declared **unilateral** independence.

Somaliland has limited self-governance, although the federal Somali government has no enforceable control over the region. Under the constitution of 1997, the region's clans established a power-sharing system that allocates seats in the legislature to ensure proper representation. Reforms made in the early 2000s aimed at creating a party-based system of governance rather than clan-based by introducing multiple political parties. The president is elected by popular vote, and observers have found elections to be fair and free. Although the region has maintained stability despite ongoing conflict in Somalia, forces have clashed with Puntland to the east, a Somali region with which Somaliland has territorial disputes. The Somaliland government has been accused of providing support and safe haven for al-Shabaab leaders, and Puntland has accused the government of assisting al-Shabaab in

Ahmed M. Mahamoud Silanyo

destabilizing the region. International organizations have found links between the president, Ahmed M. Mahamoud Silanyo, and Islamist groups.

elections in recent years but has also dealt with unrest during times of political transition. As a result, the country's economy and living standards remain low.

Some states, such as Mauritius, overcame divisions and unrest to form multiparty governments. Tanzania, though struggling with high poverty, has relatively reliable political freedom. After decades of authoritarian rule, Kenya transitioned peacefully to democracy, although protests in the mid-2000s threatened to throw the country into turmoil.

In Uganda and Sudan, a lack of political freedom accompanies extreme human rights violations. Homosexuality is illegal in Uganda, and child labor is common in the tobacco industry. The conflict with the Lord's Resistance Army, discussed in the next section, has created a humanitarian crisis in the north, with large numbers of displaced persons throughout the country. The government is considered extremely corrupt, and the security services have been accused of torturing dissidents.

Sudan, a dictatorship, is highly restrictive. President al-Bashir purged the upper ranks of the military shortly after taking power in 1989 in a bid to quell any possibility of another coup. His willingness to use violence for political means has not waned. Violence in Darfur, a region in the west of Sudan, has caused hundreds of thousands of refugees and numerous deaths at the hands of government forces.

Non-State Actors

In some cases, eastern Africa's instability is caused in part by non-state actors. The region is home to infamous groups like al-Shabaab and the Lord's Resistance Army. These groups have posed considerable challenges to local governments, carrying out attacks on civilians and terrorizing populations.

Islamist group al-Shabaab is based primarily in Somalia, although it has carried out attacks in Kenya and against foreign bases in Somalia. Al-Shabaab is affiliated with al-Qaeda and was once part of Somalia's Islamic Courts Union, a group that fought against the country's Transitional Federal Government in 2006. The group is also suspected of having ties to the separatist government in the northwestern Somaliland region, where it's thought that al-Shabaab's leaders find safe haven. Other Islamist groups, including the ISIS-linked Jahba East Africa, are also active in the region. Jahba East Africa has drawn supporters from Kenya, Uganda, Somalia, and Tanzania and has called for members of al-Shabaab to join its group.

But Islamist groups are not the only ones active in the region. The Lord's Resistance Army (LRA) is just one rebel group that has sowed instability in eastern Africa, but it is one of the most brutal and well known. Started in the 1980s by Alice Lakwena, the LRA is based in northern Uganda. It also has a presence in South Sudan, CAR, and the Democratic Republic of Congo. The group is led by Joseph Kony, who became famous in 2012 when a viral internet campaign demanded he be brought to justice for a host of war crimes. He remains at large.

The LRA started as a religiously inspired resistance group but has evolved into one of the most violent groups in Africa. The LRA has carried out numerous massacres that have killed thousands and displaced even more. The group is able to use ethnic divisions and economic instability to its benefit, positioning itself as the opposition to the government.

The LRA's tactics include crimes against humanity, such as sexual violence and the use of child soldiers, whom they kidnap and force to take part in atrocities. In order to control the children, they will make their captives take part in an act of extreme violence, sometimes against the children's own family members, and use their sense of guilt to maintain loyalty. They target civilians and use fear to control the areas of northern Uganda where they hold influence. Operating primarily in rural areas, the LRA is able to carry out its attacks with little accountability due to isolation. Although peace talks have started, Kony refuses to follow through with them, and in 2007, he executed his deputy for taking part in them.

The lack of strong governance in the region allows groups like al-Shabaab and the LRA to continue operating. Standing in direct opposition to the government, these groups are able to draw recruits from populations that feel abandoned by their leaders. Despite their extreme violence and international efforts to bring them to justice, they continue to operate with few consequences.

Ethnic Conflict

Ethnic conflict has also played a large role in political instability in eastern Africa. Like the rest of Africa, eastern Africa is home to many linguistic and ethnic groups, as well as religious sects. There are many reasons why violence breaks out between these groups. In some cases, it is due to resource scarcity: when there is limited access to water or food, groups sometimes clash over scarce resources. In Africa, the legacy of colonialism also plays a role. Colonial powers often favored one or more ethnic groups over others, leaving a societal hierarchy that was not there before. Other times, the government itself will aggravate ethnic tension with favoritism or by seizing power.

Conflicts between ethnic groups have taken place in several eastern African countries, including Kenya in 2007 to 2008 and during the South Sudanese civil war. The Rwandan genocide of

Victims of the Rwandan genocide of 1994 are pictured here. More than eight hundred thousand people were killed in the conflict.

Rwandan soldiers prepare to take part in a multistate effort to combat growing violence in CAR in 2014.

1994, however, is perhaps the best-known case of ethnic violence in recent history. As in Burundi, the Belgian government favored the wealthy Tutsis and marginalized the Hutu, two groups that differed more due to social status than ethnicity.

After independence, tensions remained high between them. In 1994, the Hutu-led government blamed the assassination of the president on the Tutsi-led Rwandan Patriotic Front. Hutu extremists encouraged the killing of the Tutsi, using media and militias to spread the violence. Identification cards, introduced by the Belgian colonial forces, were used to verify to which ethnic group victims belonged.

In just one hundred days, more than eight hundred thousand people were killed.

The genocide came to an end through the efforts of the internationally backed Rwandan Patriotic Front, but it also killed thousands as it fought to secure the country. The group also pursued the extremists that perpetrated the violence into the Democratic Republic of Congo, where fighting continued for around two decades.

In Rwanda, reconciliation has been underway ever since. The many atrocities carried out and the level of violence the country saw have made unification difficult, but the discussion of ethnicity is now illegal in the country, and efforts to overcome the past are still being made. The government has been accused of authoritarianism and hostility to opposition, but along with nonprofit groups, it has also overseen the difficult work of bringing a deeply fractured country back together.

Regional Relations

Relations between eastern African states are, in some cases, extremely tense. Eritrea and Ethiopia have a history of conflict, and Sudan and South Sudan still have a complicated relationship after South Sudan became an independent country. Somalia and Ethiopia fought against one another in the 1970s, and Djibouti and Eritrea have engaged in conflict along their shared border. Tanzania and Rwanda have poor relations, and Kenya does not have strong relations with Somalia. This is in part due to Somalia's inability to effectively contain al-Shabaab, which has been carrying out attacks in Kenya in recent years.

Tanzania, Kenya, and Uganda are closely aligned and have considerable trade agreements. The three founded

Wangari Maathai

Wangari Maathai was a political and environmental activist born in rural Kenya in 1940. After studying biology in the United States and Germany, she returned to Kenya and received her doctorate at the University of Nairobi, becoming the first woman in eastern or central Africa to do so. She became active in women's rights groups in the 1970s, becoming chairwoman of the National Council of Women of Kenya. She then went on to found the Green Belt Movement, an organization that uses environmental initiatives to support women's empowerment and community development. In 2004, Maathai was awarded the Nobel Peace Prize in recognition of her work. She passed away in 2011.

The Green Belt Movement is focused on Maathai's idea that by planting trees and establishing other environmental practices, communities can become economically stable and food secure. Kenya traditionally had many small farms, one in each yard. During the colonial era, such practices were banned, forcing the public to become reliant on markets that were often far from their homes. The Green Belt Movement helps reestablish local agriculture and promotes community economic growth through projects like honey manufacturing. The organization also assists communities in planting trees. Her work helped women across Kenya secure economic freedom and become politically active.

Wangari Maathai was a Kenyan political leader and founder of the environmental Green Belt Movement, which empowers communities and women.

The East African Community is a regional group that promotes cooperation among member states, leaders of which are pictured above.

the East African Community, an organization that has facilitated greater trade between them and helped strengthen cooperation between Kenya and Uganda. Historically, Kenya and Uganda are linguistically and culturally similar, and continued strong relations have been seen as vital to strengthening the regional economy.

In 2016, a proposed oil pipeline project highlighted the tension between regional states. The pipeline, financially backed by the United States, is intended to run from Uganda to the Indian Ocean, but deciding on the route has been difficult. States involved, including Somalia and Tanzania, have struggled to find a planned route that will be safe from possible attacks by non-state actors.

World Relations

Most states in East Africa have established strong relations with the international community, although Sudan is an exception. China, the United States, Russia, and the European Union are all very active in the region, as are humanitarian organizations and the United Nations. Djibouti, a coastal country, is favored by foreign militaries due to its stable governance. It is home to the United States' largest military base on the continent.

Sudan has been largely marginalized by the international community due in part to the continued conflicts around the country, including Darfur. The government has also been accused of funding the Lord's Resistance Army and other non-state actors. President al-Bashir is currently wanted by the International Criminal Court on charges of war crimes and crimes against humanity, and when he leaves the country he could be arrested. International warrants, however, must be enforced by governments, and so far al-Bashir has not been held accountable. In 2015, he traveled to South Africa, but after briefly barring him from returning to Sudan, the South African government allowed him to leave the country. The following year he traveled to Uganda, where the government again let him leave without arrest.

Nelson Mandela was one of the leaders of South Africa's African National Congress and a key figure in ending apartheid.

5 | Southern Africa

S
outhern Africa rests at the very bottom of the continent, bordering the Atlantic and Pacific Oceans. The countries that make up the region are Angola, Botswana, Lesotho, Malawi, Mozambique, Namibia, South Africa, Swaziland, Zambia, and Zimbabwe. Of those, South Africa is the most influential in the region.

While other regions in Africa share commonalities in governance, southern Africa is extremely politically diverse. Governments in the region include absolute monarchies and fully democratic states, with just about every shade of the political spectrum in between represented. Development and human rights are also varied, and the region has some of the most highly ranked states on the Ibrahim Index and some of the lowest. Many of the states in southern Africa are completely stable and have been for decades. Others have overcome extreme hardship and unrest, and some have become authoritarian, repressive states.

Among other issues, the region has struggled with the legacy of apartheid left by colonial rule. Under colonial rule, majority black populations were ruled over by the white minority, with the power structure kept in place through racist discriminatory laws. Dismantling that legacy was a significant hurdle to democracy in several regional states, including South Africa.

Colonization

Although much of southern Africa was controlled by the British until the mid-1900s, other European powers were present in the region as well. In Angola, the Portuguese began establishing coastal trade posts in the sixteenth century and gradually took control of the interior in the nineteenth century. The same process started in Mozambique much earlier; the Portuguese arrived on the coast in 1505 but did not formally establish a colony there until 1752.

Soldiers from Rhodesia, now Zimbabwe, fought with the British in World War I.

The Dutch were present in southern Africa during the seventeenth century, particularly in what would become South Africa. During war with Britain in the 1800s, the Dutch lost control of their colony in South Africa, called Cape Colony. But there is still a substantial Dutch legacy in the area. The Afrikaners of South Africa are those with Dutch heritage, and although a minority, there is a white population of natural-born citizens in the country. Prior to the end of apartheid, the term "Boer" was more commonly used than "Afrikaner."

Most states in the region became independent in the 1960s, with the exception of Namibia, which became a sovereign state in 1991. South Africa became independent in 1961, but the apartheid government remained in place until

1994. In his autobiography, famed activist Nelson Mandela reflected on the effects of colonialism on something as fundamental as his name:

> On the first day of school, my teacher, Miss Mdingane, gave each of us an English name and said that from thenceforth that was the name we would answer to in school. This was the custom among Africans in those days and was undoubtedly due to the British bias of our education. The education I received was a British education, in which British ideas, British culture, British institutions, were automatically assumed to be superior. There was no such thing as African culture. Africans of my generation—and even today—generally have both an English and an African name. Whites were either unable or unwilling to pronounce an African name, and considered it uncivilized to have one. That day, Miss Mdingane told me that my new name was Nelson. Why she bestowed this particular name upon me I have no idea. Perhaps it had something to do with the great British sea captain Lord Nelson, but that would be only a guess.

Malawi and Zambia were granted independence in 1964, with Zimbabwe following a year later. Botswana and Lesotho became independent in 1966, and Swaziland declared independence in 1968. Mozambique and Angola became independent in 1975.

In southern Africa, where many white settlers remained following independence, colonialism has a lasting legacy. The domination of the black population by the white minority has perhaps had the longest-lasting effect on politics. Both Zimbabwe and South Africa saw nationalist forces fight against white control, though today the two countries are governed in extremely different ways.

Government Structures

Following independence, various forms of government were established by southern African countries. Most became presidential democracies, with legislatures and elections. However, some chose different forms of government or have evolved into authoritarian regimes. Some are monarchies, while others hold regular elections with smooth transitions of power. While all states have unique governance to some degree, in many regions their commonalities are significant, be it in terms of government structure or their level of political freedom. This makes the level of diversity among governments in southern Africa particularly remarkable.

In Lesotho, the prime minister serves as the head of state and government, with a king serving as a functional and ceremonial figurehead much as the monarchies of Europe do. Lesotho's prime minister, Pakalitha Mosisili, underscored his hopes for stability when he was elected in 2015. Mosisili follows Prime Minister Thomas Thabane, who now lives in South Africa after a coup attempt. Mosisili told journalists, "We owe it to our people to give them a stable government," adding, "There will be parliamentary reform, and there will be constitutional reform for that matter."

Unlike Lesotho, Swaziland is an absolute monarchy. Although the state originally adopted a constitution that put in place a government similar to that of Lesotho, the king dissolved it and retains all power. The country does have elections for some representatives in the parliament, but the king appoints all high-ranking officials and the judiciary.

Several states in the region are considered authoritarian. Angola, despite having a president as head of government, does not have elections. Instead, the majority party elected to parliament appoints its leader to the position. All power is held by the president, and Jose Eduardo dos Santos has held the office since 1979. Zimbabwe, where Robert Mugabe has held the presidency since 1980, is perhaps the least democratic in the region, with numerous human rights abuse accusations and highly active state security forces that carry out political violence.

According to the *New York Times*, Mugabe plans to hold the presidency until his death. Journalists Hopewell Chin'ono and Norimitsu Onishi observe:

> When Mr. Mugabe—the world's oldest head of state—celebrated his 92nd birthday here over the weekend [February 2016], his advancing age and visible frailty focused attention on the increasingly fierce struggle within his party to succeed him. The jockeying for power, always a subterranean theme at the annual bashes, was too much for Mr. Mugabe to ignore.
>
> Blaming "senior party members" motivated by "their own evil interests"— as well as the British and the Americans for sowing divisions within his party—Mr. Mugabe said: "Factionalism, factionalism, and, I repeat, factionalism has no space. It has no place at all in our party."
>
> ... Mr. Mugabe, who said recently that he will govern "until God says 'come,'" has already announced his intention to run for re-election in 2018.

Many are concerned about the power vacuum that Mugabe could leave when he dies; the in-fighting between party members occurring while Mugabe is still alive points to potential problems down the road for Zimbabwe's stability.

But southern Africa is also home to many stable, vibrant political systems. South Africa, after a prolonged battle against apartheid, has emerged as one of the strongest nations on the continent and a global power. Namibia, which became an independent state from South Africa in 1990, transitioned smoothly to democracy. Botswana has been a stable democracy since gaining independence in 1966. Mozambique and Zambia, despite some electoral flaws and oppression of dissidents and opposition, have been found to have credible elections.

Apartheid was in place in South Africa from 1948 to 1994. Protests against the racially segregated government are pictured here.

Apartheid

The apartheid government in South Africa was established in 1948. It was abolished in 1994, following years of struggle by nationalist groups and leaders, including Nelson Mandela. Apartheid was an institutionalized form of racism that segregated the black majority population while ensuring power remained with the white minority.

Apartheid, though introduced formally in 1948, was part of South African politics for centuries. The Dutch and the British maintained a strict racial **caste system**. This caste system functioned much like a class system by consolidating wealth and power in the hands of white settlers. The government controlled where black South Africans could live and work, as well as how they were taught, the quality of their medical care, and other public services (which were not as good as those offered to white citizens). In 1969, only white citizens were allowed to vote.

The apartheid government put in place a system of land distribution that forced black South Africans to live on one of ten homelands. Four of these homelands were declared independent by the government, and residents lost South African citizenship. Residents on the other homelands were legally not considered South African; the government considered homeland residents as illegal immigrants. This affected their freedom of movement and representation in South Africa. Although autonomous, they had no economic infrastructure and were set up in a way that made governance nearly impossible. Therefore, they remained largely under South African control. The international community never recognized the homelands as independent states.

There was strong domestic resistance to apartheid within South Africa, led by the African National Congress (ANC). A nationalist organization, the group began advocating for a more radical agenda in 1949. The organization staged demonstrations and other mass protests, including strikes and civil disobedience campaigns. It also violently clashed with government forces, and in 1960 police killed sixty-nine people during one protest. Shortly after the violence, the government began targeting the ANC, arresting leaders and those suspected of helping the group.

In 1961, the ANC established uMkhonto we Sizwe (or MK), a militant wing that began carrying out attacks against the government. The wing was established by Nelson Mandela, who went on to lead the ANC and become the first president of postapartheid South Africa. MK engaged in guerrilla warfare with the government, working toward freedom. The group was classified by international powers as a terrorist group due to its campaign of bombings and attacks, but later the ANC and Mandela were recognized for bringing about the end of apartheid.

Political Instability

With the exception of Angola and Zimbabwe, most of southern Africa has become relatively politically stable. Some protests in South Africa in recent years have led to clashes with authorities, but by and large the political systems in the region are strong and able to govern. In the cases of Angola and Zimbabwe, the state is very strong. However, the authoritarian nature of the ruling regime can lead to instability, as seen in the 2011 Arab Spring uprisings in other parts of the continent.

Political stability is complex and interacts with every other facet of governance. On one hand, the mere presence of a strong state does not suggest that a country is stable. In Zimbabwe, the strong central state is maintained through violent repression of the people, which can eventually destabilize the government if the people as a whole challenge the state's authority. While in some cases, such as Egypt in

This statue commemorates tribal chiefs in Botswana, where tribal traditions are an important part of civic life.

northern Africa, this leads to the ruler stepping down, and in cases like Libya, the state can essentially collapse.

States like Botswana, however, have a record of stability that stands out on the continent. The country has experienced multiple transitions of power, during which unrest can occur, without incident or violence. South Africa is also stable and has never experienced a coup, something few states in Africa can claim.

Corruption, which is high in states like Malawi and Mozambique, can also threaten stability. Corrupt governments often neglect crucial issues in favor of personal gain or rewarding supporters. This can increase inequality. Inequality, in turn, can lead to protests and pressure on the government.

Kgotla

Botswana has been one of southern Africa's most stable countries. While this is thanks to many factors, including economic strength, one factor stands out: the tradition of equality and democracy. In Botswana's villages, the *kgotla* system has long served as a way to rule and mediate disputes. The system even includes courts of law. A tribal leader, called a *Kgosi*, convenes a public meeting, where important matters to the community are decided. This tribal system remains in place today and is able to function alongside the state. In fact, the coexistence of traditional tribal authority structures and the government has helped Botswana maintain political legitimacy and stability. Today, many Kgosi, or chiefs, are lawyers, who are able to provide accurate legal and political guidance to their people.

Kgotla is an opportunity for everyone involved to discuss an issue or decision in order to come to a consensus. It is based in the country's tradition of *morero*, or consultation, a value that the government continues to advocate today. Botswana also values an old Setswana saying, "The highest form of war is dialogue," which points to its belief in resolving issues through conversation rather than violence. The president will call a kgotla together over key issues, allowing people to ask him questions, and provide feedback much like a town hall. Because of this, and the long-standing tradition of such communal governance, Botswana considers itself one of the oldest democracies in the world.

In Namibia, a separatist movement in the northeast briefly threatened the stability and unity of the country in the late 1990s. The Caprivi Strip is a border region inhabited by Lozi, an ethnic group with populations in Angola, Botswana, Zambia, and South Africa. In 1994, three years after Namibian independence, the Caprivi Liberation Army (CLA) was formed with the mission of fighting for autonomy. By 1998, the group was clashing with Namibian forces, and in 1999, the CLA launched a full wave of attacks against Namibian military and police targets in the region. The Namibian government responded immediately with military forces and arrests and ended the uprising quickly. In 2002, the region declared independence, although it is not recognized by any other government. Despite Namibia's peaceful political history, tensions remain high in the northeast so long as reconciliation is not pursued.

Development

Just like the many differences in the political systems of southern Africa, development levels are also across the spectrum. The region is home to some of the most developed countries in Africa and some of the least developed in the world.

Angola, Lesotho, Malawi, Mozambique, and Zambia are all on the United Nations' list of least developed countries. Despite unrest and political repression, positive development has been seen in Zimbabwe, where President Mugabe has launched pro-development initiatives in recent years. Mozambique is the lowest in human development for the region, ranking 180 out of 188. Malawi, Lesotho, Zimbabwe, Swaziland, and Angola are also considered as having low human development.

Vendors like these, in the Mozambique town of Aldeia Biri-Biri, are common in southern Africa, where development is varied.

South Africa is considered a developed country, rather than a developing country, despite high inequality and significant poverty. Although South Africa has a strong infrastructure and a developed economy, the state also has significant social issues that must be addressed.

Many countries in the region have seen remarkable economic growth in recent years. Yet that growth does not necessarily help development. Mozambique, despite being ranked low on development, has one of the highest GDP growth rates in the region. Botswana has also seen rapid economic growth in the twenty-first century, and Angola is one of the fastest-growing economies in the world. But in many countries, the wealth has yet spread to the people.

Political Freedom and Human Rights

Political freedom is, on average, significantly more established in southern Africa than in other regions. In most states, elections are considered credible even if tampered with, meaning that although there are some process flaws, the end result reflects the will of the people. Although the region saw several civil wars in the latter half of the twentieth century, the twenty-first century has been primarily calm.

On the other hand, human rights violations are rife, particularly in Zimbabwe. The government in Zimbabwe has been accused of violating almost every basic human right internationally mandated, including the rights to food and shelter, as well as freedom of movement. Mass graves have been found across the country, and many are believed to contain the bodies of President Mugabe's political opponents.

Zambia's government cracks down often on those who criticize the government and restricts freedom of the press. In Malawi, excessive use of force by police and security officials, as well as poor prison conditions, have raised concerns among international observers. In Lesotho, where decades of guerrilla warfare and coups have undermined the government's authority, sexual violence and child labor are common. Angola has an extremely low standard of life, with one of the lowest life expectancies and highest infant mortality rates in the world.

Regional Relations

South Africa is the dominant country in the region and has strong trade relations with neighboring states. Namibia and South Africa have strong economic relations, but tension does exist between the two, given the history of South African

Nelson Mandela

Nelson Mandela was a politician and political activist born in 1918. As a core member and eventually the leader of the African National Congress, he was instrumental in ending the apartheid state in South Africa. In 1961, he helped establish the ANC's militant wing, called the uMkhonto we Sizwe (MK) and urged the ANC toward more direct action against the government's discriminatory policies. The following year he was arrested and sentenced to life imprisonment for conspiracy to overthrow the state. Mandela served twenty-seven years of his sentence before an international campaign secured his release in 1990. Upon his release, Mandela helped negotiate an end to apartheid. After the end of apartheid, he became the country's first non-white president in 1994. He passed away in 2013.

Mandela is remembered today as a hero, but he wasn't always seen as one. He and the ANC were once considered terrorists due to the guerrilla warfare the group carried out against the South African government. While in prison in the 1980s, he became known for his antiapartheid stance and soon became the face of the liberation movement. He received the Nobel Peace Prize in 1993, along with the last apartheid president Frederik Willem de Klerk, in recognition of the work they did to bring about peace. Mandela is considered the father of democracy in South Africa.

Nelson Mandela was arrested in the early 1960s for his involvement in the ANC's military wing; he was released in 1990.

rule in Namibia. There have been no significant wars fought between southern African states, with most conflict focused internally or as wars for independence.

All states in southern Africa are members of the Southern African Development Community (SADC), an organization that works to build economic relations and social cooperation between regional states, which it refers to as "Regional Integration." According to the SADC, its mission includes nearly every facet of life in southern Africa:

> The main objectives of Southern African Development Community (SADC) are to achieve economic development, peace and security, and growth, alleviate poverty, enhance the standard and quality of life of the peoples of Southern Africa, and support the socially disadvantaged through Regional Integration. These objectives are to be achieved through increased Regional Integration, built on democratic principles, and equitable and sustainable development.

The organization includes states that border the region, such as Madagascar and Tanzania. The SADC began as a way for groups working for independence to coordinate in the 1960s and 1970s, although it wasn't formally established until 1980. The group has been criticized by some international organizations, including Human Rights Watch, for not enforcing human rights standards among member states.

World Relations

Economic ties also govern southern Africa's relations with the world. Most states in the region have strong ties to the United

States, Europe, and Asian powers. South Africa has voiced interest in becoming a permanent member of the United Nations Security Council, the most powerful body in the organization. Its interest in doing so underlines its growing global influence and importance as one of the most powerful countries in Africa.

Zimbabwe does not have strong relations with the international community and has been sanctioned by the United States and its allies. China remains close to Zimbabwe due to extensive trade deals, but other world leaders have called for President Mugabe to be tried for war crimes by the International Criminal Court. Mugabe has responded by calling for Africa to establish its own court, in which to try Europeans. In 2016, Mugabe made headlines when he was awarded a Chinese peace prize, called the Confucius Peace Prize, though he did not accept the award when he learned it had not come from the Chinese government. News of the award sparked renewed criticism of Mugabe's human rights violations.

CorpsAfrica is an organization that places Africans in underserved communities in their own countries, similar to the Peace Corps.

6 The Future of Politics in Africa

The decades since independence have been difficult for Africa, with the vast majority of states experiencing unrest, coups, and political turmoil. Civil war, genocide, and corruption have further undermined governance, making it difficult for many states to meet the needs of their people. However, in the past decade, Africa has emerged as one of the fastest-growing economic regions in the world. Rapid changes on the continent are having an impact on the politics of numerous states.

Whether it's the Arab Spring in northern Africa or educated youth pushing for changes in sub-Saharan Africa, the future of politics in Africa will be driven by individuals taking an active role in governance. Yet there are also a few key concerns that could create more problems for politics in Africa, including climate change and extremism. There is much work that must be done if Africa will be able to capitalize on its considerable potential. Establishing stable and democratic governance will require a great deal of work for some states.

Given Africa's recent history of unrest, current trend of rapid growth, and the many factors at play in the continent's political development, it is difficult to say with certainty what the coming decades could bring. The lessons of the Arab

Spring in northern Africa were clear: seemingly unchangeable political situations can shift overnight, including dictatorships. Africa has a young population with higher rates of education and greater access to technology than their parents. This could mean that the continent is heading into an era of increased democratization. But Africa remains largely underdeveloped, and the weight of **urbanization** and climate change could make governments less efficient, further undermining governance.

In this chapter, we'll discuss some of the dominant trends that point to a bright future for African politics and some of the issues that must be dealt with if strong governance is going to take root on the continent.

Reconciliation

Conflict has been one of the most significant issues in African politics in the decades since independence, undermining governments and reinforcing tension between ethnic or religious groups. Ending conflicts, such as those between factions in South Sudan or CAR, is crucial to establishing strong governance. Yet reconciliation is just as important. In South Africa, the postapartheid state focused on reconciling the black population and the minority white population, and by so doing likely avoided an armed conflict between the two. In Rwanda, establishing peace after the 1994 genocide took many years of ongoing counseling, reconciliation programs, and discussion of what took place. Although never easy, reconciliation is the first step in knitting a war-torn country back together.

In the years after independence, the impact that long-term tension between groups can have on governance became clear. This effect was seen when warring factions struck out at one

Rwanda has worked hard to reconcile following the 1994 genocide. Here, a man sits with a woman he targeted during the conflict.

another in a bid for power. Many states experience these kinds of power struggles after conflict; power vacuums open up space for one dominant group to take control. Often these dominant groups repress those they feel will try to take power away from them. Reconciliation allows for post-conflict states to transition to democracy, as Namibia did after its war for independence, without ongoing strife. But it requires groups to address the tensions that once led to conflict, tensions like ethnic divisions or ongoing discrimination. Reconciliation must be accompanied by reform that seeks to remedy these problems.

The need for meaningful reform and reconciliation can be seen in Nigeria, where militants have once again risen up in response to the oil industry's presence in the Niger Delta. Ongoing conflict threatens the economy and civilians, just as it did in the 1990s and early 2000s. But the government failed to address the militants' concerns then, leading to the current crisis.

Education and Technology

Education can be one of the driving forces behind political change, as we've seen in northern Africa. In Tunisia and Egypt, revolutions were led by educated youths who were frustrated with the lack of opportunity (among other concerns). With education comes a demand for inclusion in a nation's decision-making process, as well as a greater awareness of the political factors that have an impact on day-to-day life. This can include a new awareness of corruption, lack of democracy, and discrimination.

Trends in Africa, where education rates are still well below the global average, suggest that educated citizens could put significant pressure on governments to become more democratic. Higher education enrollment in sub-Saharan

Africa grew from 2.3 million in 2000 to 5.2 million in 2010, and African states spend more on education proportionally than any other region in the world. An estimated 59 percent of twenty- to twenty-four-year-olds in Africa will have a secondary education by 2030, a 17 percent jump from 2015.

But there is still a great deal of inequality across the continent. While in South Africa and Zimbabwe literacy is between 90 and 100 percent, in Chad the literacy rate is just 39 percent. In the Central African Republic and Mali, populations struggle to attend school regularly due to unrest. South Sudan's education rates are some of the worst in the world, with low primary school enrollment and significantly fewer opportunities for female students. These vast differences underline the fact that not all African states are the same, which is why it's difficult to discuss African politics in broad strokes. Countries rocked by conflict remain far behind other African nations. The factors that could totally reshape African politics in the coming decades do not come into play in these countries. At times, conflict makes survival a country's primary concern.

Education isn't the only thing that's changing civil society in Africa, though. Technology has taken Africa by storm, with tech investment growing more and more each year. Cell phones in particular are changing the way Africa works. Mobile phone ownership rates are high across the region; in sub-Saharan Africa, two-thirds of homes have at least one. Mobile phone ownership has changed economics across the region, with money transfers via phone hitting the continent long before they were available in the United States. This has allowed families to keep their money more secure in dangerous areas, which in turn can help increase stability. If money is secure, non-state actors and criminals lose one of their income sources.

Cell phones have changed the lives of Africans across the continent, influencing everything from economics to politics.

Cell phones also offer easy access to social media, which can be a huge driver of change in politics. Social media allows people across continents and oceans to communicate instantly, sharing ideas and news without using a middleman (which might be controlled by the government). Opposition groups, such as Zimbabwe's Movement for Democratic Change, and activists are able to use social media to communicate with citizens inside the country. In Tanzania, the Civic United Front has used sites like Facebook to help coordinate a network of activist websites and training programs to engage and train young people.

For protesters and organizers, social media sites like Twitter and WhatsApp are crucial to staying in touch, sharing updates on safety concerns, and making sure the rest of the world is aware of what is taking place. Awareness can pressure the government to halt crackdowns or bring international pressure for leaders to reform or resign.

Urbanization

African cities have been growing at significant rates for years, with no signs of slowing down. The continent is home to four megacities, referring to cities with more than ten million residents, and several more are expected to emerge in the coming decade. The United Nations has estimated that urban populations in sub-Saharan Africa will double before 2030, due to both migration and population growth.

Urbanization can lead to economic growth, development, and political stability as the middle class grows and the economy adjusts to a more intertwined system of supply and demand. City populations require efficient policy to ensure needs like housing, food, and health care are easily filled. In developing countries, when these needs aren't met illicit activities and black markets can fill in the government's gaps and slums can proliferate.

Urban residents are on average more educated than rural residents, and if managed well, cities can lead to a rise in the middle class. When these two key areas of change are present (increased education and a growing middle class), often democratic reform is achieved. People with more disposable income and free time become involved in politics and have a greater understanding of their rights. A stronger economy and more stable middle class can also cut down on the number of uprisings and protest that threaten governments. Although it can take time depending on development, cities can transform countries and their governments. In Tanzania, Dar es Salaam is growing amid an economic boom, and the government is being proactive in developing key industries to meet the needs of the people.

But many countries in Africa have raised concern that they cannot deal with rapid urbanization. The Sudanese capital of Khartoum is one of the continent's quickly growing cities, and the government has struggled with underdevelopment, conflict, and inequality. Failure to adequately govern urban centers can contribute to increased crime, greater inequality, poverty, and food insecurity (lack of reliable access to food). With those concerns comes the possibility of radicalization; groups like Boko Haram and ISIS are able to prey on populations that feel disenfranchised and unsupported by the state. Protests can also break out, and in some cases the unrest can throw the country into turmoil.

Extremism

While growing education, access to technology, and urbanization suggest that African governance may be moving in positive directions, there are many important issues that must be dealt with before the continent can fully become democratic. In the most vulnerable states, the threat of extremism is significant, and as the changes that are shaping the continent take place, finding ways to combat that threat are critical. In some cases, combating extremism requires opening up the political system. However, in many states where opening up the political system is most crucial, those in charge are not comfortable with making such big changes.

Extremist groups, like Boko Haram in Nigeria, the Seleka militia in CAR, and the Lord's Resistance Army in Uganda, draw on a sense of frustration among populations the government neglects. They are also able to highlight ethnic and religious differences, making it all the more important that a strong national identity be established. Although religion is often at the center of discussions of these groups, and it can sometimes play a role, in most cases groups are born out of political complaints and concerns. Religion serves as an easy and effective rallying point, can underscore a supposed lack of corruption in comparison to the government, and provides justification for actions. But in truth religion is often secondary to political motivations in extremist groups.

Discontented young people are among the most dangerous and most potentially transformational in a country, providing recruits for antigovernment groups or serving to propel the country's economy and civil society forward. In many cases, young populations are referred to as "ticking time bombs" if not properly provided for, something northern Africa saw firsthand when protests broke out in 2011.

Africa has one of the youngest populations in the world, with more than two hundred million people between the ages of fifteen and twenty-four. With current rates of population growth, that number could double before 2045, according to the UN. In 2014, youth unemployment was at a staggering 60 percent across the continent, around double the rate for non-youths. Even in stable countries the rate was high; in South Africa, the unemployment rate was almost 53 percent. If unemployment, discrimination, lack of political freedom, and other issues aren't dealt with, this young population could provide recruits for extremist and militant groups.

Biotech in Africa

Food insecurity is one of the most significant threats to governance in Africa, with potential to create instability through mass migration, famine, and discontent. But **biotechnology** experts are working to ensure that the crops of the future can meet Africa's needs without falling victim to concerns like droughts and diseases. These innovations could make the continent more resilient in the face of climate change and could produce more food to feed the many in need.

Drought-resistant crops were successfully planted in the United States in 2013, and projects were started shortly thereafter to get water-efficient crops, like maize, to Africa. The International Food Policy Research Institute estimates that the biotech breakthrough could help produce yields 17 percent higher during severe droughts in eastern Africa. Improved nutritional quality is another major breakthrough that could change the lives of those in need, producing crops with more good nutrients. This could help cut malnutrition and stretch food supplies because foods will have a higher nutrient count per serving. Similarly, meal replacement products like Plumpy'Nut have been developed to meet basic daily nutritional needs at an affordable cost, helping cut youth malnutrition in vulnerable populations. While these solutions could help change food in Africa, countries will need to look for more ways to adapt in the face of continued food insecurity.

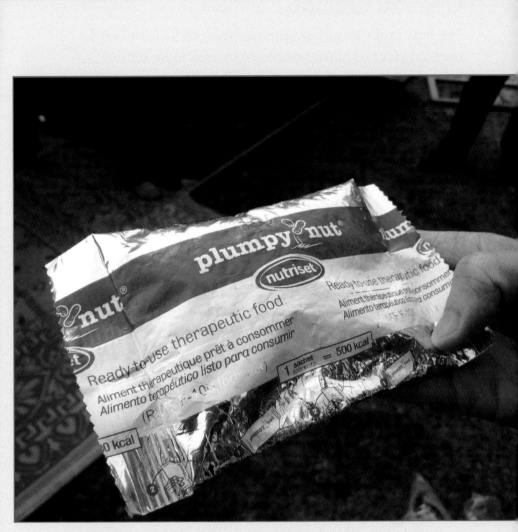

Plumpy'Nut is a calorie-dense food that aid groups distribute to people in developing countries.

Climate Change

The impact of climate change is one that will be felt around the world if governments aren't able to effectively address environmental damage. Africa is under particular threat from the effects of climate change, due to factors like widespread poverty and existing food or water insecurity. Countries across the region are poorly positioned to deal with the possible large-scale migration caused by rising sea levels and extreme weather events, and as a result, the continent as a whole is vulnerable. Even stable states, such as Botswana or Morocco, could be impacted negatively if neighboring states come under significant strain.

Countries like Kenya and Sudan have already experienced extreme droughts that heavily impacted the food supply. Food insecurity can drive populations to migrate or lead to famine, as can water insecurity. Countries in Africa already struggle with a lack of access to food and water, particularly in countries like Somalia. Climate change threatens to worsen existing insecurity, as well as impact agriculture. According to the UN, the effect of climate change could be felt in agricultural areas that depend on rain by 2020, with a 50 percent reduction in production. This will impact many impoverished countries whose economies depend on agriculture.

The political impact of climate change has many sides, but it starts with the government's ability to respond to crisis. Underdeveloped states that already struggle to meet the basic needs of their people, such as Ethiopia or CAR, will not be able to handle a lack of food, mass migration, and the many concerns that come along with such issues. These issues include increased disease, as people are living within close quarters, and malnutrition as a result of lack of food. Housing and education

Drought has had dire consequences for this family who owns livestock in Somaliland; shrinking resources have killed many of their animals.

also become concerns during mass migration, particularly in areas already impacted by large numbers of refugees.

Climate change poses a threat to political stability. The economic demand created by climate change could bankrupt already poor countries, making them more reliant on international aid and less able to meet their own financial needs. This could cause coups and uprisings, including in currently stable states not prone to such turmoil. Yet there is hope that in the future every citizen in Africa will make their voice heard. In the face of many obstacles, including potentially catastrophic changes to our planet, Africans continue to fight for representation, equality, and stability.

Regional Map of of Africa

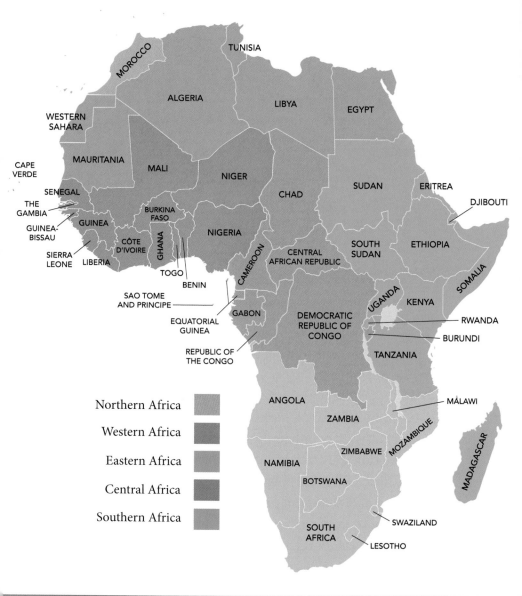

MOROCCO
TUNISIA
ALGERIA
LIBYA
EGYPT
WESTERN SAHARA
CAPE VERDE
MAURITANIA
MALI
NIGER
SUDAN
ERITREA
DJIBOUTI
SENEGAL
THE GAMBIA
CHAD
BURKINA FASO
GUINEA
GUINEA-BISSAU
SIERRA LEONE
LIBERIA
CÔTE D'IVOIRE
GHANA
NIGERIA
CAMEROON
CENTRAL AFRICAN REPUBLIC
SOUTH SUDAN
ETHIOPIA
SOMALIA
TOGO
BENIN
SAO TOME AND PRINCIPE
EQUATORIAL GUINEA
GABON
REPUBLIC OF THE CONGO
DEMOCRATIC REPUBLIC OF CONGO
UGANDA
KENYA
RWANDA
BURUNDI
TANZANIA
ANGOLA
MALAWI
ZAMBIA
MOZAMBIQUE
MADAGASCAR
ZIMBABWE
NAMIBIA
BOTSWANA
SWAZILAND
SOUTH AFRICA
LESOTHO

Northern Africa

Western Africa

Eastern Africa

Central Africa

Southern Africa

Chronology

1871–1912 The Scramble for Africa results in most of the continent becoming European colonies

1928 The Muslim Brotherhood is formed in Egypt

1956–1975 African states become independent from European colonizing powers

1961 South Africa's ANC becomes militant; Nelson Mandela is arrested

1965 The Chad civil war begins

1979 Somalia-Ethiopia War begins

1979 Teodoro Obiang takes power in Equatorial Guinea

1980 The LRA is formed in Uganda

1989 President Omar al-Bashir comes to power in Sudan

1990 Namibia becomes independent from South Africa; Nelson Mandela is released from prison

1993 Eritrea becomes independent from Ethiopia

1994 The Rwandan Genocide occurs

1994 Apartheid ends in South Africa

1996–1997 The First Congo War takes place

1998–2003 The Second Congo War takes place

2000 Civil war breaks out in Ivory Coast

2002 Daniel Moi's dictatorship ends in Kenya

2004–2007 The first Central African Republic Bush War is waged

2010 Arab Spring protests begin in Tunisia

2011 South Sudan gains independence; Muammar Gaddafi removed from power in Libya

2013 A coup in Egypt overthrows Mohamed Morsi

2014 El-Sisi is elected in Egypt after staging a coup the previous year; Boko Haram kidnaps more than two hundred schoolgirls in Nigeria

Glossary

absolute monarchy A system of government in which the royal family holds all political and legislative power.

annex To take control of a nation and add it to a country's existing territory.

apartheid The legal system of racial segregation that existed in South Africa until 1994.

Arab Spring A series of protests across Arab countries that began in December 2010.

archipelago A small chain of islands, often made up of many very small islands.

authoritarian A type of government in which power is held by one person or small group, and there are few political freedoms.

autonomy A synonym for self-government.

biotechnology A branch of science dedicated to engineering new organisms.

caste system A form of social hierarchy with strictly defined social classes.

corruption The use of government power for personal gain.

coup The sudden and illegal overthrow of an existing government, usually resulting in the group carrying out the coup taking power for itself.

diaspora A group of ethnically similar populations living in various places around the world.

dissent Sharing opinions or thoughts outside of the norm or unshared by those in power.

genocide The purposeful targeted killing of a large number of people, usually of an ethnic or religious group.

incumbent A politician who currently holds office.

Islamist Those seeking to govern according to their interpretation of Islamic law.

liberal A descriptor for an ideology based on the advocacy of civil liberties and representative government.

linguistically Referring to language, this term can mean dialects as well as completely separate languages.

martial law When a country's military holds power and normal law is suspended for a period of time.

military junta A form of military dictatorship in which the military explicitly holds on to power.

militia Small group of armed fighters, sometimes loyal to the government and other times opposed to the government.

national identity The traditions and culture that provide a sense of communal identity to citizens of a country.

politics Actions or debates related to power and governance of a nation; actions or debates that shape a nation's relationship with other countries around the world.

power vacuum The absence of a central ruling authority; a situation characterized by competition for power and often unrest.

precious metal Valuable metal, such as gold, silver, and platinum.

protectorate A country that is protected and controlled by another country; though similar to a colony, a protectorate often still has its own government in place.

referendum A vote on a particular issue.

repression The forceful subduing of certain political thoughts, actions, or ideologies by a state.

scapegoat Someone or something that can be blamed for negative events but is usually not truly responsible for the action.

sectarianism Tension or conflict between branches of the same religion or group, such as the Sunni-Shia conflict in Islam.

secular Nonreligious.

sovereignty The power or authority of a state to govern itself.

tribalism Describes a society organized around familial groups and tribal identity.

uncontested Describes an election in which no one argued with or formally complained about the results.

unilateral Describes an action taken or declaration made by one person or party.

urbanization A process that occurs when a significant portion of a population shifts from living in rural areas to living in urban areas.

Further Information

Books

Caplan, Gerard. *The Betrayal of Africa.* Toronto, Canada: Groundwood Books, 2008.

Mathabane, Mark. *Kaffir Boy: The True Story of a Black Youth's Coming of Age in Apartheid South Africa.* New York: Simon & Schuster, 1998.

Meredith, Martin. *The Fate of Africa.* London, UK: Simon & Schuster, 2011.

Rotberg, Robert I. *Governance and Leadership in Africa.* Broomall, PA: Mason Crest, 2013.

Websites

The African Union

http://www.au.int

The African Union is a continent-wide organization assisting cooperation and development among member states. All African states, except for Morocco, are members in the group, which meets regularly and issues statements from the continent as a whole.

The Council on Foreign Relations

http://www.cfr.org/projects/world/africa-program/pr1031

A leading Washington, DC, think tank, the Council of Foreign Relations' Africa Program hosts roundtables, publishes studies, and maintains a website featuring analysis on political developments on the continent. CFR profiles individuals and groups and studies governance and security in the region.

The United Nations

http://www.un.org/en/sections/where-we-work/africa/index.html

The United Nations website includes information about UN missions in Africa, development programs, and other organizations working in the region. As the leading international organization, the UN has unprecedented access to governments and civilian populations, as well as a backlog of all United Nations Security Council resolutions regarding Africa.

Bibliography

Acemoglu, Daron, and James Robinson. *Why Nations Fail: The Origins of Power, Prosperity, and Poverty*. London, UK: Random House, 2012.

Autesserre, Severine. *Peaceland: Conflict Resolution and the Everyday Politics of International Intervention*. New York: Cambridge University Press, 2014.

Bates, Robert H. *When Things Fell Apart*. New York: Cambridge University Press, 2008.

Bourne, Richard. *Nigeria: A New History of a Turbulent Century*. London, UK: Zed Books, 2015.

Campbell, John. "Africa in Transition." *Council on Foreign Relations*. Retrieved June 14, 2016 (http://blogs.cfr.org/campbell).

Chabal, Patrick, and Jean-Pascal Daloz. *Africa Works: Disorder as Political Instrument*. Bloomington, IN: Indiana University Press, 1999.

Clark, Nancy L., and William H. Worger. *South Africa: The Rise and Fall of Apartheid*. New York: Routledge, 2013.

Cooper, Frederick. *Africa in the World: Capitalism, Empire, Nation-State*. Cambridge, MA: Harvard University Press, 2014.

Davidson, Basil. *The Black Man's Burden: Africa and the Curse of the Nation-State*. New York: Random House, 1992.

Foster, Douglas. *After Mandela: The Struggle for Freedom in Post-Apartheid South Africa*. New York: W.W. Norton & Co, 2012.

Fraihat, Ibrahimi. *Unfinished Revolutions: Yemen, Libya, and Tunisia After the Arab Spring*. New Haven, CT: Yale University Press, 2016.

French, Howard W. *A Continent for the Taking: The Tragedy and Hope of Africa*. New York: Random House, 2005.

Gasiorowski, Mark, David Long, and Bernard Reich, eds. *The Government and Politics of the Middle East and North Africa*. Boulder, CO: Perseus, 2014.

Gourevitch, Philip. "The Life After." *New Yorker*, May 4, 2009 (http://www.newyorker.com/magazine/2009/05/04/the-life-after).

Jeffrey, James. "Somaliland's Search for Place." *Foreign Affairs*, May 26, 2016 (https://www.foreignaffairs.com/articles/somalia/2016-05-26/somalilands-search-place).

Lemarchand, Rene. *Burundi: Ethnic Conflict and Genocide*. New York: Cambridge University Press, 1995.

Mamdani, Mahmood. *When Victims Become Killers: Colonialism, Nativism, and the Genocide in Rwanda.* Princeton, NJ: Princeton University Press, 2002.

Meredith, Martin. *The State of Africa: A History of the Continent Since Independence.* London, UK: Simon & Schuster, 2013.

Meservey, Joshua. "Somalia's Governance Problem." *Foreign Affairs*, May 15, 2016 (https://www.foreignaffairs. com/articles/somalia/2016-05-15/somalias-governance-problem).

Natsios, Andrew S. "Lords of the Tribes." *Foreign Affairs*, July 9, 2015 (https://www.foreignaffairs.com/articles/ sudan/2015-07-09/lords-tribes).

Osman, Tarek. *Egypt on the Brink: From Nasser to the Muslim Brotherhood.* New Haven, CT: Yale University Press, 2013.

Prunier, Gerard. *Africa's World War.* New York, NY: Oxford University Press, 2009.

Searcey, Dionne. "Hissene Habre, Ex-President of Chad, Is Convicted of War Crimes." *New York Times*, May 30, 2016 (http://www.nytimes.com/2016/05/31/world/africa/hissene-habre-leader-chad-war-crimes.html?ref=africa&_r=0).

Stearns, Jason. *Dancing in the Glory of Monsters: The Collapse of the Congo and the Great War of Africa.* New York: Perseus Books, 2012.

Van Reybrouck, David. *Congo: The Epic History of a People.* New York: HarperCollins, 2015.

Index

Page numbers in **boldface**
are illustrations.
Entries in **boldface**
are glossary terms.

health care and education,
26, 31, 105
human rights, 12, 19, 34–37,
46, 52, 54–58, 70, 81, 85,
93, 96–97

incumbent, 50
ISIS (Islamic State), 20, 32,
38, 71, 106
Islamist, 12, 15, 17, 19–20,
32, 62, 69, 71
Ivory Coast, 28, 31, 34, 37, 39

Kenya, 61, 63–66, 70–72,
75–78, 110
Kony, Joseph, 62, 71–72

Lagos, Nigeria, **4**
Lesotho, 81, 83–84, 91, 93
liberal, 19
Liberia, 27–30, 33–37, 39, 63
Libya, 9–11, 13, 15, 18–23,
25, 38, 50, 89
linguistically, 61, 72, 78
Lord's Resistance Army,
61–62, 70–72, 79, 107

Madagascar, 61–62, 64,
67–70, 96
Malawi, 81, 83, 89, 91, 93
Mali, 22–23, 28, 31, 34,
37–39, 41, 103

Mandela, Nelson, **80**, 83,
87–88, 94, **95**
martial law, 33, 41
Mauritania, 9, 13–14, 16, 23, 25
Mauritius, 61–63, 66, 70
military junta, 31–33
militia, 10, 18, 20, 30, 40
monarchy, 5–6, 11–12, 15,
18–19, 84
Morocco, 5, 7, 9, 12–13,
15–19, 23, 110
Mozambique, 81–83, 86, 89,
91–92, **92**
Mubarak, Hosni, 17–19
Mugabe, Robert, 85–86, 91,
93, 97

Namibia, 81–82, 86, 91,
93–96, 102
national identity, 52–53
National Liberation Front
(FLN), 24
Niger, 22, 28, 33–34, 37–38, 41
Nigeria, 22, 28–29, 31–32,
34, 37–39, 102
northern Africa, 9–25

parliament, 5, 13, 17–19,
84–85
politics, 5
power vacuum, 6, 86, 102
protectorate, 11–13, 68

About the Author

Bridey Heing is a writer and book critic based in Washington, DC. She holds degrees in political science and international affairs from DePaul University and Washington University in Saint Louis, Missouri. Her areas of focus are comparative politics and Iranian politics. Her master's thesis explores the evolution of populist politics and democracy in Iran since 1900. She has written about Iranian affairs, women's rights, and art and politics for publications like the *Economist*, *Hyperallergic*, and the *Establishment*. She also writes about literature and film. She enjoys traveling, reading, and exploring Washington, DC's, many museums.